HONEST TO GOD

365-DAYS OF
PERSONAL DEVOTION

Stephen Martin

HONEST TO GOD: 365 DAYS OF PERSONAL DEVOTION

Copyright © 2020
One Church Resource
171 FM 3219
Harker Heights, TX 76548
onechurchresource.com

Editors: Lindsey Oswald, Ignaseio Cattlin, Joshua Brown, May Campbell
Cover & Layout Design: Rebecca Leach

Printed in the United States of America
All rights reserved under International Copyright Law.

SPECIAL THANKS

Thank you, Lindsey Oswald and Rebecca Leach, for doing the heavy lifting with the content, editing, and design. Also, a special thanks to those who helped write the daily devotions: May Campbell, Joshua Brown, and Ignaseio Cattlin.

NAME:

START DATE:

CONTACT IF LOST OR STOLEN:

TABLE OF CONTENTS

INTRODUCTION
Whole Heart Devotion

> And you will seek Me and find Me, when you search for Me with all your heart.
>
> Jeremiah 29:13

The human heart weighs less than a pound (450g). It beats 100,000 times a day and over 2.5 billion times in the average lifetime. Your system of blood vessels – arteries, veins, and capillaries – is over 60,000 miles long – enough to go around the world more than twice.

This is not just a fantastic spectacle; it is the 'heart' of human life. Without your heart, your body would quickly cease to work. You can live without a lot of things, but your heart isn't one of them.

Did you know that the Bible has a lot to say about your heart? It's difficult to read the Bible without this constant reference to people's heart or the heart of a person. Why is that? It's because, in scripture, **the heart is a metaphor for the inner life**.

> God blesses those whose hearts are pure, for they will see God.
>
> Matthew 5:8

When you see heart referenced in scripture, it is the center and the source of your whole life – thinking, feeling, and willing. It's the seat of the physical, spiritual, and mental life.

This is sometimes very difficult for us to understand as westerners because we live in a moralist and individualistic society. We tend to see our life in compartments, one area of our lives separated from the others, but in scripture, the heart refers to all of us: spirit, soul, and body.

Jesus had a way of using parables that would challenge us to look at our life as a whole. Many times Jesus would be asked a question, and he would tell a story and respond with another question. Why? Because Jesus always taught to the heart. It was his signature move, and it was very effective.

> The people were amazed at his teaching, for he taught with real authority—quite unlike the teachers of religious law.

> Mark 1:22

Jesus emphasized and focused on the inner life. For example, Jesus rebuked the religious leaders of Israel for focusing on looking righteous instead of being righteous on the inside.

> "What sorrow awaits you teachers of religious law and you Pharisees. Hypocrites! For you are like whitewashed tombs— beautiful on the outside but filled on the inside with dead people's bones and all sorts of impurity.

> Matthew 23:27

In Matthew, chapter 5, Jesus challenges what people thought was good when He speaks beyond one's actions to the condition of their heart.

> "You have heard the commandment that says, 'You must not commit adultery.' But I say, anyone who even looks at a woman with lust has already committed adultery with her in his heart.

> Matthew 5:27-28

"You have heard that our ancestors were told, 'You must not murder. If you commit murder, you are subject to judgment.' But I say, if you are even angry with someone, you are subject to judgment! If you call someone an idiot, you are in danger of being brought before the court. And if you curse someone, you are in danger of the fires of hell.

Matthew 5:21-22

Why did Jesus do this? Because Your life flows from your heart. We tend to focus on the outside, but Jesus knew everything good or bad comes from our heart.

Above all else, guard your heart, for everything you do flows from it.

Proverbs 4:23

Perhaps the most well known passage of Jesus speaking to the heart is found in Matthew chapter 22 when Jesus was asked, "Which is the greatest commandment in all of the Torah and prophets."

Jesus replied, "'You must love the Lord your God with all your heart, all your soul, and all your mind.' This is the first and greatest commandment. A second is equally important: 'Love your neighbor as yourself.' The entire law and all the demands of the prophets are based on these two commandments."

Matthew 22:37-40

In this passage, we see the secret to whole heart devotion. Simply put, it is to love God above everything else and with our entire self. When God is first, it is easy to love our neighbor and live the life God has called us to live as Christians.

We have created this resource to help you grow closer to God each day through intentional personal devotion. By following this simple but powerful template, you will grow closer to God and His plan for your life.

THE ESSENTIALS
Of Whole Heart Devotion

WORSHIP

But the time is coming—indeed it's here now—when true worshipers will worship the Father in spirit and in truth. The Father is looking for those who will worship him that way. For God is Spirit, so those who worship him must worship in spirit and in truth."

John 4:23-24

Many people think that worship is the ten or fifteen minutes we spend singing songs at church or the latest album from our favorite Christian band, but it is so much more than that. When we talk about "worship", many of us have different ideas of what worship is! For some of you, you may think back to a moment in your childhood where you stood behind a pew reading music of a book. Or, for others, you might remember the moment during a service where God spoke to you and met you where you were. But I'm sure most of us associate worship with a particular segment of service where we use music to glorify God. But **worship is far more than something we do**: it's the positioning and the posture of our hearts.

Throughout scripture, we see the words "worship" and "praise appear. Most of the translations we read today use these two words, but they mean so much more in their original languages. When we look at the many translations of the words "worship" and "praise," we see that worship is so much more than singing to God on a Sunday morning.

1.   **Worship is about giving worth to God.**

When we enter into a time of worship, we take time to show God that he is worth it. He's worth our attention, our time, and our focus. His ways are way bigger and way better than ours. The Hebrew word for this definition of worship is "barak," which means "to kneel, to bow, to bless." We see this form of worship in Genesis 24, when Abraham's servant, Laban, bows down to worship God.

> "Then I bowed low and worshiped the LORD. I praised the
> LORD, the God of my master, Abraham, because he had led me
> straight to my master's niece to be his son's wife.

> Genesis 24:48d

God is worth our affection and praise. A physical way to walk out this type of worship is by coming to God on our knees. When we do this, it's about blessing God and humbling ourselves underneath his authority.

2. Worship is about surrender.

Not only do we show God that he's worth our worship, but we surrender our lives to him every time we worship him. Whether it's our first time surrendering to him, or our one-hundredth time, we give our situations and circumstances to him. Another translation of the word "praise" is the Hebrew word "yadah", which means "to shoot, to cast, to throw, or to lift up." This Hebrew word appears in 2 Samuel 22:

> For this, O Lord, I will praise you among the nations; I will
> sing praises to your name.

> 2 Samuel 22:50

Surrendering to God is about waving the "white flag" of our lives to God. When we surrender, we give God full control of the outcome and rely fully on him. One way we can physically engage with this idea is by lifting our hands up towards God. In doing this, we not only let God take control, but we also position ourselves to receive what he has in store.

3. Worship is about the posture of our heart.

Worship shouldn't just be "Simon Says," and it shouldn't be generic. It can often feel this way when we sing the same songs and hear the same lines over and over. But God makes it clear that the worship he honors comes from an authentic place in our hearts. Our last Hebrew translation for "praise" is the word "tehillah", which means "to sing." Again, this form of worship isn't just reading the words of a hymnal or a projector; worshiping God this way is about positioning our hearts to glorify him.

Yet you are holy, enthroned on the praises of Israel.

Psalm 22:3

This verse shows us that God inhabits the praises of his people. When we posture our hearts towards him, we set ourselves up to spend time with him.

One way we can practice this is by putting all distractions aside. If that means getting up early before the kids are awake or silencing your cell phone: God wants us to be fully devoted to him when we worship. You may even close your eyes to slow down your thoughts and relax your mind. Either way, having the right posture before God is what sets us up to receive his presence and his blessings.

Each day you will be challenged to focus on God by being intentional about putting a few minutes aside at the start of each day to posture your heart to hear from Him.

BIBLE STUDY

"and so, dear brothers and sisters, I plead with you to give your bodies to God because of all he has done for you. Let them be a living and holy sacrifice—the kind he will find acceptable. This is truly the way to worship him. Don't copy the behavior and customs of this world, but let God transform you into a new person by changing the way you think. Then you will learn to know God's will for you, which is good and pleasing and perfect."

Romans 12:1-2

God transforms our life by changing the way we think. Many of us focus on behavior modification, but that won't be enough; why? Because of the way God changes you is inside out. This process of learning to think like God is called Sanctification. It starts when we surrender our lives to Christ and continues as we learn the will of God and practice His ways.

The Apostle Paul, when writing to the church at Thessalonica, primarily of Greek influence, helps us understand how this process works.

May God himself, the God of peace, sanctify you through and through. May your whole spirit, soul, and body be kept blameless at the coming of our Lord Jesus Christ.

1 Thessalonians 5:23

Paul is helping those in this church understand how to think differently about their life. They were used to seeing everything from the outside in. This is natural for us because we naturally judge a book by its cover and a person by their actions, but our actions are the result of how we think. Our spirit is the part of us that connects with God, and before we surrendered to Jesus, it was dead.

> When Adam sinned, sin entered the world. Adam's sin brought death, so death spread to everyone, for everyone sinned.

> Romans 5:12

However, when we surrender our lives to Jesus, John 3:3 says we are born again and can now connect with God and live according to His ways. It is from our spirits now, not our soul body (the flesh), that we can thrive in every area of our life.

> The message of the cross is foolish to those who are headed for destruction! But we who are being saved know it is the very power of God.

> 1 Corinthians 1:18

So, how do we learn how do we think like God? **God changes the way you think through His Word, the Bible.**

> For the word of God is alive and powerful. It is sharper than the sharpest two-edged sword, cutting between soul and spirit, between joint and marrow. It exposes our innermost thoughts and desires.

> Hebrews 4:12

I am amazed when I see Christian people abandon God's Word in the name of being Christian. **We follow Jesus, and He is God's Word.**

> So the Word became human and made his home among us. He was full of unfailing love and faithfulness. And we have seen his glory, the glory of the Father's one and only Son.

> John 1:14

> All Scripture is inspired by God and is useful to teach us what is true and to make us realize what is wrong in our lives.

It corrects us when we are wrong and teaches us to do what is right. God uses it to prepare and equip his people to do every good work.

2 Timothy 3:16-17

Many Christians don't know God because they don't know His Word, the Bible. Many people don't make time to study God's Word or when they do read the Bible; they find it difficult to understand. But you can understand the Bible. It is the foundation of our faith.

Three Tips When Reading the Bible:

1. **Read it as a story about God, not you.** Don't look at it as a to-do list. Ask yourself what you learned about who God is, what his character is. It isn't self-help. Ask the Holy Spirit to show you more about God.

2. **Read it as it was meant to be read.** Don't read it out of context. Look around what you're reading and leave your opinions aside.

    The Bible is like the director's cut of a movie, with all of the extras and a lot of things going on. Who wrote it, style, purpose, who is it wrote too. What kind of book is it? Get a study Bible.

3. **Read it all.** Not just 140 characters at a time! Don't jump to conclusions. Read Scripture as it was meant to be read. It is one story about God, told in 66 books. It is helpful to read the Bible from start to finish each year.

Hermeneutics is the study of how to interpret the Bible. Here are **three basic rules of hermeneutics** that can help you understand what you read:

First, **interpret scripture with scripture**. When scripture seems to contradict itself, it doesn't. Stay humble and seek to understand the passage. A study Bible can help you understand the basic context of the passage. Many times as you continue to read, the meaning will become clearer.

Next, **interpret unclear passages with clear passages**. For example, don't scream where Scripture whispers or whisper where Scripture screams. The Bible, like many ancient texts, uses repetition to emphasize the importance of a principle or behavior.

Finally, **ask if the passage is descriptive or prescriptive**. Sometimes the Bible is just describing what happened but not what you should do. For example, King Solomon married many wives, but that doesn't mean God told him to. As a matter of fact, God specifically said that kings should not have multiple wives, and Solomon's disobedience led Him away from God's best.

As you engage God through His Word, the Bible, we have created a daily plan that goes through the whole Bible in Chronological order. Take the time each day to read the entire Bible to grow closer to God and to see the many facets of his character.

PRAYER

> Now in the morning, having risen a long while before daylight, He went out and departed to a solitary place and there He prayed.

> Mark 1:35

If Jesus is our model for how to live our lives, we should look closely at what the Bible has to say about the teachings of Jesus about prayer and His own prayers. Over and over again in the Gospels, we see Jesus taking time to spend with the Father in prayer. And, if He needed that kind of workout discipline, how much more do we need it?

> And when He had sent the multitudes away, He went up on the mountain by Himself to pray.

> Matthew 14:23

In His longest recorded sermon, Jesus emphasizes prayer and how important it is to us as his followers. He also tells us practically how to pray.

> "And when you pray, do not be like the hypocrites, for they love to pray standing in the synagogues and on the street corners to be seen by others. Truly I tell you, they have received their reward in full. But when you pray, go into your room, close the door and pray to your Father, who is unseen. Then your Father, who sees what is done in secret, will reward you.

> Matthew 6:5-6

Here we see that Jesus tells us that prayer is not about being religious or being seen by others, but it is about knowing God the Father who is unseen.

Prayer is also to be a regular part of the Christian life. So why don't more people pray? Many times it's because they aren't sure how. One of the things I love about Jesus is how he always taught to the heart and made it practical for everyone to follow. In what many call the Lord's Prayer, Jesus gives his followers a simple but effective template for prayer.

Below is a simple and effective template that you can use when you pray. It follows the Lord's Prayer found in Matthew 6:9-13. We have also included several other prayer models seen in Scripture in the Resources section in the back of this devotional.

> Pray like this: Our Father in heaven, may your name be kept holy. May your Kingdom come soon. May your will be done on earth, as it is in heaven. Give us today the food we need, and forgive us our sins, as we have forgiven those who sin against us. And don't let us yield to temptation, but rescue us from the evil one.

> Matthew 6:9-13

Remember, prayer is simply talking to God, and it is all about relationship. Both knowing God and being known by God. The Lord's Prayer gives us a framework that emphasizes **four key essentials of prayer**.

1. **Start with worship.** Acknowledge that God is holy, good, and trustworthy. God's perspective is higher than your perspective.

2. **Then surrender your life or circumstance.** Lay aside what you think should happen and recognize that God's way is best. An easy way to think about this is to put into God's hands what you can't control while being open and honest with what you can control.

3. After worship and surrender, **make your requests.** With confidence, make your request, and thank God for His answer. Just like a parent, God loves to give to his children. Remember, nothing is too small for God. He wants to hear it all from you, personally. Every four weeks, you will complete personal prayer targets that will help guide your prayer requests.

4. **Reflect on your life and relationships.** Give forgiveness and pray for others to forgive. God takes forgiveness seriously, and it is a requirement,

not a suggestion. The quickest way to cut off God's voice from your life is by harboring unforgiveness in your heart.

Pray for protection. Ask God to protect you from temptation and confess His Word over your life. You and I need God's supernatural protection from the dangers around us, both physical and spiritual.

As you prioritize daily prayer, you will grow closer to God and learn how to hear his voice when you need it in your life the most. Complete the monthly prayer targets and requests located in the Appendix. We have also included other Biblical prayer models in the Appendix you can use during your time of personal devotion. A powerful addition to prayer is the Biblical practice of fasting. We have also included an introduction to fasting in the Appendix.

COMMUNITY

> Now to him who is able to do immeasurably more than all we ask or imagine, according to his power that is at work within us,

> Ephesians 3:20

Your faith is personal, but it isn't private. So many Christians struggle in their relationship with God because they lack a Christian community. You need other people in your life on a daily and weekly basis who share your faith and walk alongside you as you grow.

So what does community look like practically? **Jesus gives us community through His Spiritual Family, the Local Church.** As you connect in the church, you will realize that it is a greenhouse for spiritual growth.

> I had to feed you with milk, not with solid food, because you weren't ready for anything stronger. And you still aren't ready,

> 1 Corinthians 3:2

Our spiritual growth is similar to our physical growth. We all start in this journey of following Jesus as spiritual babies, but as time goes on, and we grow closer to God and closer to each other, we continue to grow more and more mature.

Christian community is not possible without God AND others.

The Community of God is a result of God's work within us. To the extent that we personally experience God's work in our lives and our commitment to the family, we experience belonging.

How does this work? The process starts when we give our lives to Jesus and continues as we continue to surrender our life to him in a process called Sanctification, or the process of how we become more like the Jesus we read about in the Bible.

Christian community is not possible without unity. CommUNITY is made possible only through unity. Jesus says in Matthew 12 that a house divided against itself cannot stand. Amos 3:3 Can two people walk together without agreeing on the direction? The apostle Paul describes the church as a body, and he emphasizes that a healthy body is unified.

> But our bodies have many parts, and God has put each part just where he wants it. How strange a body would be if it had only one part! Yes, there are many parts, but only one body. The eye can never say to the hand, "I don't need you." The head can't say to the feet, "I don't need you."
>
> 1 Corinthians 12:18-21

Christian Community attracts the presence of God.

> How good and pleasant it is when God's people live together in unity! It is like precious oil poured on the head, running down on the beard, running down on Aaron's beard, down on the collar of his robe. It is as if the dew of Hermon were falling on Mount Zion. For there the Lord bestows his blessing, even life forevermore.
>
> Psalm 133: 1-3 NIV

There is a lot of poetic language here but hear what is being said. Everything flows from God, the head, and when we live together in unity, our lives carry the presence of God, and his power and presence gets on our whole life. Not just at church, but everywhere we are. **Unity marked the early church.**

> They worshiped together at the Temple each day, met in homes for the Lord's Supper, and shared their meals with great joy and generosity—all the while praising God and enjoying the

goodwill of all the people. And each day, the Lord added to their fellowship those who were being saved.

Acts 2:46-47

The values of God's Kingdom are different from the values of the world. The culture of the early church stood in contrast to that of the world. When the culture and values of the world seeped in, it caused disunity in the Christian community. This is the reason for most of Paul's letters to the early churches:

> Don't copy the behavior and customs of this world, but let God transform you into a new person by changing the way you think. Then you will learn to know God's will for you, which is good and pleasing and perfect.

Romans 12:2

We are to be in this world but not of this world. We are to love and engage this world, but our culture is not to be marked by the same values of this world.

> Do not love this world nor the things it offers you, for when you love the world, you do not have the love of the Father in you. For the world offers only a craving for physical pleasure, a craving for everything we see, and pride in our achievements and possessions. These are not from the Father, but are from this world. And this world is fading away, along with everything that people crave. But anyone who does what pleases God will live forever.

1 John 2:15-17

It is in Christian community that we are transformed and equipped to make an eternal impact in our world. Each day as you prioritize relationships with other Christians, you will encourage and be encouraged to live out your faith with more authenticity and boldness than ever before. Every seven days, you will be challenged to reflect on and record the time you spent with other Christians.

THE DAILY JOURNAL

DAY 1

Worship

Get alone with God. Find a quiet place. Sit down. Silence all distractions.

Scripture: Genesis (1)(2)(3)

As you read today, notice how God pursues Adam and Eve even though they are hiding from Him. They sinned, and they lied to Him, but he still shows them grace and mercy because that's who He is!

Prayer

What is God saying to you? What do you need to say to God? Use a prayer model and your monthly prayer targets and requests as a guide.

DAY 2

Worship

Get alone with God. Find a quiet place. Sit down. Silence all distractions.

Scripture: Genesis (4)(5)(6)(7)

In today's reading, we see God's instructions to Noah for building the boat. Notice the details that He gives Noah. God didn't miss anything. He's in the details and at work to restore fallen humanity in relationship with Himself.

Prayer

What is God saying to you? What do you need to say to God? Use a prayer model and your monthly prayer targets and requests as a guide.

DAY 3

Worship
Get alone with God. Find a quiet place. Sit down. Silence all distractions.

Scripture: Genesis (8) (9) (10) (11)
In today's reading, pay attention to the complexities of God's character. He is love, but he also blesses and curses his enemies. We all start off distant from God, but he pursues all of us, just like he pursued Adam and Eve.

Prayer
What is God saying to you? What do you need to say to God? Use a prayer model and your monthly prayer targets and requests as a guide.

DAY 4

Worship
Get alone with God. Find a quiet place. Sit down. Silence all distractions.

Scripture: Job (1) (2) (3) (4) (5)
As you read today, notice that despite the loss and trauma Job experiences, he remains faithful as a servant of God. It would have been easy for Job to curse God, but he shows us that God is worthy of praise and can be trusted even in our hardest times.

Prayer
What is God saying to you? What do you need to say to God? Use a prayer model and your monthly prayer targets and requests as a guide.

DAY 5

Worship
Get alone with God. Find a quiet place. Sit down. Silence all distractions.

Scripture: Job ⑥ ⑦ ⑧ ⑨
In today's reading, we see Job's intimate relationship with God. Despite what he's been through, Job still cries out to Him. We see that even though God is great and powerful, He also lends Himself to be intimate with mankind.

Prayer
What is God saying to you? What do you need to say to God? Use a prayer model and your monthly prayer targets and requests as a guide.

DAY 6 ✓

Worship
Get alone with God. Find a quiet place. Sit down. Silence all distractions.

Scripture: Job ⑩ ⑪ ⑫ ⑬
Today in Job 11:6, Jobs' friend, Zophar, says, "God exacts of you less than your guilt deserves." While much of what Jobs' friends are telling him is not wise counsel, Zophar makes a true statement about how merciful God is. We all receive the mercy of God, just by living.

Prayer
What is God saying to you? What do you need to say to God? Use a prayer model and your monthly prayer targets and requests as a guide.

DAY 7 ✓

Worship
Get alone with God. Find a quiet place. Sit down. Silence all distractions.

Scripture: Job (14) (15) (16)
In today's reading we will see that Job begins to struggle and doubt God's goodness, but he still recognizes God's sovereignty in Job 14:5: "Since his days are determined, and the number of his months is with you, and you have appointed his limits that he cannot pass." This is a great reminder for us, and for Job, that God is always in control, and that brings us comfort because He is trustworthy.

Prayer
What is God saying to you? What do you need to say to God? Use a prayer model and your monthly prayer targets and requests as a guide.

COMMUNITY

I attended a church service this week (circle):   YES   NO

I shared my faith and talked about my church with others this week (circle):   YES   NO

I connected with other Christians in a smaller group this week. If yes, describe.

DAY 8 ✓

Worship
Get alone with God. Find a quiet place. Sit down. Silence all distractions.

Scripture: Job ⑰ ⑱ ⑲ ⑳
In today's reading, we see God's redeeming nature. To redeem means to "buy back", and Job has faith that God will redeem his situation and that even if it is the end of his life, it's not the end of his story.

Prayer
What is God saying to you? What do you need to say to God? Use a prayer model and your monthly prayer targets and requests as a guide.

DAY 9 ✓

Worship
Get alone with God. Find a quiet place. Sit down. Silence all distractions.

Scripture: Job ㉑ ㉒ ㉓
As you read today, think about the difference between mercy and grace. We so often use these words interchangeably, but they are actually very different. Mercy is when we don't get what we do deserve, when we are spared a punishment, while grace is when we get what we don't deserve. As humans born into sin, we all receive God's mercy. Everything above and beyond that which is good is grace!

Prayer
What is God saying to you? What do you need to say to God? Use a prayer model and your monthly prayer targets and requests as a guide.

DAY 10 ✓

Worship

Get alone with God. Find a quiet place. Sit down. Silence all distractions.

Scripture: Job (24) (25) (26) (27) (28)

In today's reading, we see God in the wisdom He has given Job. In Job 27:6 he says, "I hold fast my righteousness and will not let it go; my heart does not reproach me for any of my days." Job shows us how we can feel the emotions of grief and even anger without mistrusting God's motives.

Prayer

What is God saying to you? What do you need to say to God? Use a prayer model and your monthly prayer targets and requests as a guide.

DAY 11 ✓

Worship

Get alone with God. Find a quiet place. Sit down. Silence all distractions.

Scripture: Job (29) (30) (31)

As you read today, notice how Job considers God a friend. Friendships are built on intimacy and trust, and we see that even though Job is struggling to feel God's presence at the moment, he knows that it's possible to experience that level of intimacy with Him.

Prayer

What is God saying to you? What do you need to say to God? Use a prayer model and your monthly prayer targets and requests as a guide.

DAY 12 √

Worship
Get alone with God. Find a quiet place. Sit down. Silence all distractions.

Scripture: Job ㉜ ㉝ ㉞
In today's reading, imagine being Job, and after losing everything, you are misunderstood by your friends, and you don't know what to do next. Job is in pain, physically and emotionally. Still, Job knows that he's not alone, and he shows us that even in our suffering, we can suffer in a way that still honors God.

Prayer
What is God saying to you? What do you need to say to God? Use a prayer model and your monthly prayer targets and requests as a guide.

DAY 13 √

Worship
Get alone with God. Find a quiet place. Sit down. Silence all distractions.

Scripture: Job ㉟ ㊱ ㊲
As you read today, consider how easy it is to feel like we don't need God when things are going well for us. How often do we forget to praise Him, thank Him, and lean on Him until we are in a spot where we realize we need Him? It's always easier to have faith in God during our trials when we practice having faith in Him during the good times!

Prayer
What is God saying to you? What do you need to say to God? Use a prayer model and your monthly prayer targets and requests as a guide.

DAY 14 ✓

Worship

Get alone with God. Find a quiet place. Sit down. Silence all distractions.

Scripture: Job (38) (39)

Today, we finally see God respond to Job. As you read, notice how God doesn't necessarily answer Jobs' questions, but He still draws near to Job and reminds him who He is.

Prayer

What is God saying to you? What do you need to say to God? Use a prayer model and your monthly prayer targets and requests as a guide.

COMMUNITY

I attended a church service this week (circle):   YES   NO

I shared my faith and talked about my church with others this week (circle):   YES   NO

I connected with other Christians in a smaller group this week.
If yes, describe.

DAY 15

Worship
Get alone with God. Find a quiet place. Sit down. Silence all distractions.

Scripture: Job ⑩ ④ ④
In today's reading, notice God's heart for restoration. We see Him not only bless Job and return to him what he had lost, but we also see for the first-time females named in family lineage.

Prayer
What is God saying to you? What do you need to say to God? Use a prayer model and your monthly prayer targets and requests as a guide.

DAY 16

Worship
Get alone with God. Find a quiet place. Sit down. Silence all distractions.

Scripture: Genesis ⑫ ⑬ ⑭ ⑮
In today's reading, we see God make a covenant with Abram. God is showing Abram that he is committed to the promise he makes that Abram will have a son. God is a promise maker, and that we can put our trust in Him!

Prayer
What is God saying to you? What do you need to say to God? Use a prayer model and your monthly prayer targets and requests as a guide.

DAY 17 √

Worship
Get alone with God. Find a quiet place. Sit down. Silence all distractions.

Scripture: Genesis (16) (17) (18)
God's mercy is on display in today's reading. Sarah took matters into her own hands, and the result was the offspring of Hagar and Abram being enemies of God's people. Despite her failings, God tells Sarah He will bless her and confirms that she will be the mother of Abram's son. He gives us what we don't deserve!

Prayer
What is God saying to you? What do you need to say to God? Use a prayer model and your monthly prayer targets and requests as a guide.

DAY 18 √

Worship
Get alone with God. Find a quiet place. Sit down. Silence all distractions.

Scripture: Genesis (19) (20) (21)
As you read today, notice God's heart for forgiveness. God tells Abraham to pray for Abimelech, even though he stole Abraham's wife. Abraham obeyed, and as a result, God healed Abimelech, his wife, and their slaves. God uses His people to show his heart for forgiveness to a broken world!

Prayer
What is God saying to you? What do you need to say to God? Use a prayer model and your monthly prayer targets and requests as a guide.

DAY 19 ✓

Worship
Get alone with God. Find a quiet place. Sit down. Silence all distractions.

Scripture: Genesis ㉒ ㉓ ㉔
God is so faithful, and he hears our prayers. Today we see Abraham's servant praying for God to send a woman for him to take back to Isaac, and before he even finished praying, Rebekah appears at the well. God is fulfilling his promise to Abraham has not been an easy journey, but step by step He has remained faithful and He can be trusted!

Prayer
What is God saying to you? What do you need to say to God? Use a prayer model and your monthly prayer targets and requests as a guide.

DAY 20 ✓

Worship
Get alone with God. Find a quiet place. Sit down. Silence all distractions.

Scripture: Genesis ㉕ ㉖
As you read today, notice how God doesn't favor people in positions of honor or respect. Instead, he favors the opposite! Whether it's the younger sibling, the needy, or the least advantaged, God shows us how to place others above ourselves.

Prayer
What is God saying to you? What do you need to say to God? Use a prayer model and your monthly prayer targets and requests as a guide.

DAY 21 √

Worship
Get alone with God. Find a quiet place. Sit down. Silence all distractions.

Scripture: Genesis (27) (28) (29)
In today's reading we will see that Job begins to struggle and doubt God's We see in today's reading that God's sovereignty covers all things, including the sins of man, or in this case, the sin and manipulation committed by Rebekah. No matter the mistakes we make or the intentional wrongdoings, we can't stand in the way of God's desired outcome!

Prayer
What is God saying to you? What do you need to say to God? Use a prayer model and your monthly prayer targets and requests as a guide.

COMMUNITY

I attended a church service this week (circle):   YES   NO

I shared my faith and talked about my church with others this week (circle):   YES   NO

I connected with other Christians in a smaller group this week. If yes, describe.

DAY 22 ✓

Worship

Get alone with God. Find a quiet place. Sit down. Silence all distractions.

Scripture: Genesis ㉚ ㉛

We see a lot of sin and jealousy in today's reading. Leah and Rachel are envious of each other and seem to be competing for Jacob's favor. This scripture shows us that even we've sinned, God is kind and provides for his flawed children, which includes all of us!

Prayer

What is God saying to you? What do you need to say to God? Use a prayer model and your monthly prayer targets and requests as a guide.

DAY 23 ✓

Worship

Get alone with God. Find a quiet place. Sit down. Silence all distractions.

Scripture: Genesis ㉜ ㉝ ㉞

In today's reading, we see God change Jacob's heart, as well as his name. This is the first of many times we will see the name Israel. God doesn't give up on Jacob, and he doesn't give up on us!

Prayer

What is God saying to you? What do you need to say to God? Use a prayer model and your monthly prayer targets and requests as a guide.

DAY 24 √

Worship

Get alone with God. Find a quiet place. Sit down. Silence all distractions.

Scripture: Genesis ㉟ ㊱ ㊲

As you read chapter 37, notice how Reuben steps in as an older brother to save Joseph's life. While his motives may have included restoring his own relationship with his father, Reuben's act gives us a picture of Jesus, our older brother who spared our lives so that we can be restored to our Father.

Prayer

What is God saying to you? What do you need to say to God? Use a prayer model and your monthly prayer targets and requests as a guide.

DAY 25 √

Worship

Get alone with God. Find a quiet place. Sit down. Silence all distractions.

Scripture: Genesis ㊳ ㊴ ㊵

As you read today, remember that not all scripture is prescriptive; much of it is descriptive. The story of Tamar, and Judah is one full of sin and manipulation. While what they did is certainly not endorsed, we still see God's faithfulness. Later in scripture, we see Judah, Tamar, and Perez listed in the lineage of Jesus. Even though they were broken people, he kept his promise to their family!

Prayer

What is God saying to you? What do you need to say to God? Use a prayer model and your monthly prayer targets and requests as a guide.

DAY 26 √

Worship

Get alone with God. Find a quiet place. Sit down. Silence all distractions.

Scripture: Genesis (41) (42)

God's generosity is on display in today's reading. He uses Joseph to warn Egypt about the famine, despite Egypt being a land that doesn't honor him. Then we see that Joseph is generous to his brothers. This is a reflection of God's generosity and favor to Joseph and the favor he received from God.

Prayer

What is God saying to you? What do you need to say to God? Use a prayer model and your monthly prayer targets and requests as a guide.

DAY 27 √

Worship

Get alone with God. Find a quiet place. Sit down. Silence all distractions.

Scripture: Genesis (43) (44) (45)

In today's reading, we see the freedom that only comes from knowing and trusting in God. He is at work in all things and helps us to forgive those who have sinned against us! Not only did God give Joseph freedom, but we will see today how Joseph then forgives his brothers for their sins against him.

Prayer

What is God saying to you? What do you need to say to God? Use a prayer model and your monthly prayer targets and requests as a guide.

DAY 28 ✓

Worship
Get alone with God. Find a quiet place. Sit down. Silence all distractions.

Scripture: Genesis (46) (47)
In today's reading, look for how God provides for His people. Even though they are in the land of their enemies during a famine, they draw near to God and His plans for them.

Prayer
What is God saying to you? What do you need to say to God? Use a prayer model and your monthly prayer targets and requests as a guide.

_____

_____

_____

COMMUNITY

I attended a church service this week (circle):   YES   NO

I shared my faith and talked about my church with others this week (circle):   YES   NO

I connected with other Christians in a smaller group this week.
If yes, describe.

_____

_____

_____

DAY 29 ✓

Worship

Get alone with God. Find a quiet place. Sit down. Silence all distractions.

Scripture: Genesis ㊽ ㊾ ㊿

Look for prophecies about Jesus in today's reading. Jacob blesses Judah, even though he is not the first-born son. This resembles the image of Jesus, who laid down his life to share the inheritance of a relationship with God with us!

Prayer

What is God saying to you? What do you need to say to God? Use a prayer model and your monthly prayer targets and requests as a guide.

DAY 30 ✓

Worship

Get alone with God. Find a quiet place. Sit down. Silence all distractions.

Scripture: Exodus ① ② ③

In today's reading, notice how God uses broken people! Moses was raised in the home of someone who wanted him dead, and later, he commits murder. God specializes in using people who aren't perfect, just like you and me!

Prayer

What is God saying to you? What do you need to say to God? Use a prayer model and your monthly prayer targets and requests as a guide.

DAY 31 √

Worship

Get alone with God. Find a quiet place. Sit down. Silence all distractions.

Scripture: Exodus ④ ⑤ ⑥

In today's reading, look for God's reassuring and compassionate nature. Moses begins to doubt himself, but God reminds him of who He says he is.

Prayer

What is God saying to you? What do you need to say to God? Use a prayer model and your monthly prayer targets and requests as a guide.

DAY 32 √

Worship

Get alone with God. Find a quiet place. Sit down. Silence all distractions.

Scripture: Exodus ⑦ ⑧ ⑨

In today's reading, we see God's patient nature. He works step by step towards His plan, even though He could have taken a much quicker approach with Pharaoh. We usually want things to happen on our own time, but God's timing is perfect, and He is with us in the waiting.

Prayer

What is God saying to you? What do you need to say to God? Use a prayer model and your monthly prayer targets and requests as a guide.

DAY 33 ✓

Worship
Get alone with God. Find a quiet place. Sit down. Silence all distractions.

Scripture: Exodus (10) (11) (12)
Today, we read about the creation of Passover, where God spares the lives of the Israelites and not the Egyptians. As you read today, remember to view God's power as a comfort, and not something to actively fear.

Prayer
What is God saying to you? What do you need to say to God? Use a prayer model and your monthly prayer targets and requests as a guide.

DAY 34 ✓

Worship
Get alone with God. Find a quiet place. Sit down. Silence all distractions.

Scripture: Exodus (13) (14) (15)
On display in today's reading is God's great love for Israel and how He fights for them. When you love something, you're willing to go to war against anything that threatens what you love, and God is willing to go to war for His people.

Prayer
What is God saying to you? What do you need to say to God? Use a prayer model and your monthly prayer targets and requests as a guide.

DAY 35

Worship
Get alone with God. Find a quiet place. Sit down. Silence all distractions.

Scripture: Exodus (16) (17) (18)
In today's reading, we see God command His people to rest, or take a sabbath. Notice how He is testing their mentality; will they have a scarcity mindset or trust that God will continue to provide for them if they stop to rest?

Prayer
What is God saying to you? What do you need to say to God? Use a prayer model and your monthly prayer targets and requests as a guide.

_____

_____

_____

COMMUNITY

I attended a church service this week (circle):   YES   NO

I shared my faith and talked about my church with others this week (circle):   YES   NO

I connected with other Christians in a smaller group this week.
If yes, describe.

_____

_____

_____

DAY 36 √

Worship
Get alone with God. Find a quiet place. Sit down. Silence all distractions.

Scripture: Exodus (19) (20) (21)
In today's reading, God gives Moses the Ten Commandments. Notice how the first five commandments are vertical, or how to honor God, while the last five are horizontal and are about honoring others. We also see a whole chapter (21) about God's desire to protect life, including life in the womb.

Prayer
What is God saying to you? What do you need to say to God? Use a prayer model and your monthly prayer targets and requests as a guide.

DAY 37 √

Worship
Get alone with God. Find a quiet place. Sit down. Silence all distractions.

Scripture: Exodus (22) (23) (24)
As you read today, notice how even though God is protective of His people, He also makes it clear that they need to show kindness even to their enemies. God gives us grace and mercy, and He expects that we give it to others!

Prayer
What is God saying to you? What do you need to say to God? Use a prayer model and your monthly prayer targets and requests as a guide.

DAY 38 √

Worship
Get alone with God. Find a quiet place. Sit down. Silence all distractions.

Scripture: Exodus (25) (26) (27)
Today's reading shows us how God wants to be near to His people. Even though they have rebelled against Him and sinned, He wants to dwell with them. Nothing we do can separate us from Him!

Prayer
What is God saying to you? What do you need to say to God? Use a prayer model and your monthly prayer targets and requests as a guide.

DAY 39

Worship
Get alone with God. Find a quiet place. Sit down. Silence all distractions.

Scripture: Exodus (28) (29) √
As you read today, don't worry about trying to understand all of the details, but focus on the purpose of what God is doing. God is pursuing His people and making a way for them to draw near to Him!

Prayer
What is God saying to you? What do you need to say to God? Use a prayer model and your monthly prayer targets and requests as a guide.

DAY 40

Worship

Get alone with God. Find a quiet place. Sit down. Silence all distractions.

Scripture: Exodus (30) (31) (32)

Today, we will read a lot about sacrifices and offerings. Notice that God is creating a way for us to atone for our sins. He wants to be in relationship with us He has a plan for us!

Prayer

What is God saying to you? What do you need to say to God? Use a prayer model and your monthly prayer targets and requests as a guide.

DAY 41

Worship

Get alone with God. Find a quiet place. Sit down. Silence all distractions.

Scripture: Exodus (33) (34) (35)

As you read today, consider how God is both loving and just. He spends some time telling Moses things about Himself, the loving qualities that we tend to focus on, but He also reminds Moses that sins have generational consequences. This can be hard to hear sometimes but remember that we want to serve a God who blesses the righteous and punishes the guilty.

Prayer

What is God saying to you? What do you need to say to God? Use a prayer model and your monthly prayer targets and requests as a guide.

DAY 42

Worship

Get alone with God. Find a quiet place. Sit down. Silence all distractions.

Scripture: Exodus (36) (37) (38)

As you read today, remember how God is with us in the every day, the mundane, and the routine. Lean into Him and praise Him, even on the days when you don't feel His presence!

Prayer

What is God saying to you? What do you need to say to God? Use a prayer model and your monthly prayer targets and requests as a guide.

COMMUNITY

I attended a church service this week (circle):   YES   NO

I shared my faith and talked about my church with others this week
(circle):   YES   NO

I connected with other Christians in a smaller group this week.
If yes, describe.

DAY 43

Worship

Get alone with God. Find a quiet place. Sit down. Silence all distractions.

Scripture: Exodus ⑨ ④⓪

Today we close out the book of Exodus. When we started, they were slaves in Egypt, and since then, we've watched the Israelites as they've wandered in the desert. They've doubted God and complained about Him, but He's been faithful and provided for them along the way.

Prayer

What is God saying to you? What do you need to say to God? Use a prayer model and your monthly prayer targets and requests as a guide.

DAY 44

Worship

Get alone with God. Find a quiet place. Sit down. Silence all distractions.

Scripture: Leviticus ① ② ③ ④

As you begin reading Leviticus, remember God is perfect and Holy and he wants to draw near to His people. Leviticus may feel dry and full of law, but it's about the process of making nearness to God possible!

Prayer

What is God saying to you? What do you need to say to God? Use a prayer model and your monthly prayer targets and requests as a guide.

DAY 45

Worship
Get alone with God. Find a quiet place. Sit down. Silence all distractions.

Scripture: Leviticus (5) (6) (7)
As you read today, notice how God makes a way for everyone to be able to provide a sacrifice for their sin. Wealthier families give an animal from their flock, but families who were poor didn't have a flock to select an animal from. God gives these families the option of bringing a bird or even flour. God meets us where we are!

Prayer
What is God saying to you? What do you need to say to God? Use a prayer model and your monthly prayer targets and requests as a guide.

DAY 46

Worship
Get alone with God. Find a quiet place. Sit down. Silence all distractions.

Scripture: Leviticus (8) (9) (10)
In today's reading, notice the character of God displayed in the way Moses treats Aaron after he loses two of His sons. As we spend more time with God and get to know His character, we should become more like Him, just as Moses did!

Prayer
What is God saying to you? What do you need to say to God? Use a prayer model and your monthly prayer targets and requests as a guide.

DAY 47

Worship
Get alone with God. Find a quiet place. Sit down. Silence all distractions.

Scripture: Leviticus (11) (12) (13)
As you read today, it's important to remember that laws for cleanliness served a purpose that we wouldn't need today. For example, when people had leprosy and they were sent outside the camp, it wasn't because they were being shamed or condemned. They did this to avoid spreading these skin conditions to others, and they were still watched over by the priest. Both the healthy and unhealthy were being cared for at the same time.

Prayer
What is God saying to you? What do you need to say to God? Use a prayer model and your monthly prayer targets and requests as a guide.

DAY 48

Worship
Get alone with God. Find a quiet place. Sit down. Silence all distractions.

Scripture: Leviticus (14) (15)
Today, we read about a leprous man being healed, then he is sent to be cleansed. Notice the parallel to justification and sanctification here. Justification is when God declares us righteous when we accept Christ as our savior, while sanctification is the process of becoming more like God as we walk in relationship with Him!

Prayer
What is God saying to you? What do you need to say to God? Use a prayer model and your monthly prayer targets and requests as a guide.

DAY 49

Worship
Get alone with God. Find a quiet place. Sit down. Silence all distractions.

Scripture: Leviticus (16) (17) (18)
You may have noticed by this point that Leviticus is not the easiest book to read in the Bible! If you start to feel discouraged or disengaged as you are reading, pause, and take a moment to ask the Holy Spirit for insight and fresh eyes to see God's character in the pages.

Prayer
What is God saying to you? What do you need to say to God? Use a prayer model and your monthly prayer targets and requests as a guide.

COMMUNITY

I attended a church service this week (circle):   YES   NO

I shared my faith and talked about my church with others this week (circle):   YES   NO

I connected with other Christians in a smaller group this week. If yes, describe.

DAY 50

Worship

Get alone with God. Find a quiet place. Sit down. Silence all distractions.

Scripture: Leviticus (19) (20) (21)

In today's reading, we see an encouraging reminder from God. We've been reading a lot about laws, but in Leviticus 21:15, God says, "I am the Lord who sanctifies him." God made a way for us, He's with us and He is for us!

Prayer

What is God saying to you? What do you need to say to God? Use a prayer model and your monthly prayer targets and requests as a guide.

DAY 51

Worship

Get alone with God. Find a quiet place. Sit down. Silence all distractions.

Scripture: Leviticus (22) (23)

As you read today, you will see a lot of requirements, reminders of law, and requirements of perfection. Rather than be discouraged, consider how this serves as a reminder of our need for God in our lives. We will never be perfect, and He knows that!

Prayer

What is God saying to you? What do you need to say to God? Use a prayer model and your monthly prayer targets and requests as a guide.

DAY 52

Worship
Get alone with God. Find a quiet place. Sit down. Silence all distractions.

Scripture: Leviticus ㉔ ㉕
At the end of today's reading, we God's character in his generosity and protection of those who are poor. He calls the rich to share and let others be free of their debts. God calls us to live generously and with an open hand, just as He demonstrates in this chapter.

Prayer
What is God saying to you? What do you need to say to God? Use a prayer model and your monthly prayer targets and requests as a guide.

DAY 53

Worship
Get alone with God. Find a quiet place. Sit down. Silence all distractions.

Scripture: Leviticus ㉖ ㉗
As you read today, notice how God isn't going to give up on His people. He tells Moses about the blessings that will come if they keep their covenant with God, and also the consequence of breaking the covenant. Usually, a broken covenant meant that the deal was over. But God makes it clear that even though there will be consequences, they can always repent and turn back to Him!

Prayer
What is God saying to you? What do you need to say to God? Use a prayer model and your monthly prayer targets and requests as a guide.

DAY 54

Worship
Get alone with God. Find a quiet place. Sit down. Silence all distractions.

Scripture: Numbers (1) (2)
As we begin reading Numbers, we see God asking Moses to perform a census of all males over the age of 20 in the twelve tribes. While He doesn't say why, we do know that God is at work, building their trust and His plan for His people.

Prayer
What is God saying to you? What do you need to say to God? Use a prayer model and your monthly prayer targets and requests as a guide.

DAY 55

Worship
Get alone with God. Find a quiet place. Sit down. Silence all distractions.

Scripture: Numbers (3) (4)
As you read today, notice again that God doesn't favor those in a position of honor. Those who minister to people and those who serve people in less glamorous ways are important and needed just the same!

Prayer
What is God saying to you? What do you need to say to God? Use a prayer model and your monthly prayer targets and requests as a guide.

DAY 56

Worship
Get alone with God. Find a quiet place. Sit down. Silence all distractions.

Scripture: Numbers (5) (6)
As we end today's reading, God gives a well-known blessing for the people. Numbers 6:24-26 "The Lord bless you and keep you; the Lord make his face to shine upon you and be gracious to you; the Lord lift up his countenance upon you and give you peace." God wants to bless us and give us peace!

Prayer
What is God saying to you? What do you need to say to God? Use a prayer model and your monthly prayer targets and requests as a guide.

COMMUNITY

I attended a church service this week (circle):   YES   NO

I shared my faith and talked about my church with others this week (circle):   YES   NO

I connected with other Christians in a smaller group this week. If yes, describe.

DAY 57

Worship
Get alone with God. Find a quiet place. Sit down. Silence all distractions.

Scripture: Numbers (7)
Today's reading is only one Chapter in Numbers; you might notice it's a long and sometimes repetitive chapter! We see each of the tribes bringing an offering to the tabernacle. While this ensures that the tabernacle and its leaders are provided for, it also blesses the hearts of the givers and conforms them into the image of the God who has blessed them.

Prayer
What is God saying to you? What do you need to say to God? Use a prayer model and your monthly prayer targets and requests as a guide.

DAY 58

Worship
Get alone with God. Find a quiet place. Sit down. Silence all distractions.

Scripture: Numbers (8) (9) (10)
As you read today, notice God's generosity and mercy towards the Levites. They did nothing but doubt God, and God still pulled them close and allowed them to serve in close proximity to Him!

Prayer
What is God saying to you? What do you need to say to God? Use a prayer model and your monthly prayer targets and requests as a guide.

DAY 59

Worship
Get alone with God. Find a quiet place. Sit down. Silence all distractions.

Scripture: Numbers (11) (12) (13)
In today's reading, notice how Moses shows God's character again. His sister, Miriam, stirs up drama, and God punishes her by giving her leprosy, but Moses asks God to heal her. God grants Moses his request, even though Miriam was deserving of punishment. God gives us mercy when we least deserve it!

Prayer
What is God saying to you? What do you need to say to God? Use a prayer model and your monthly prayer targets and requests as a guide.

DAY 60

Worship
Get alone with God. Find a quiet place. Sit down. Silence all distractions.

Scripture: Numbers (14) (15) Psalm (90)
In today's reading, we see that God is a promise keeper. Despite all of their rebellion, He reminds His people that they will still receive the promises He made!

Prayer
What is God saying to you? What do you need to say to God? Use a prayer model and your monthly prayer targets and requests as a guide.

DAY 61

Worship
Get alone with God. Find a quiet place. Sit down. Silence all distractions.

Scripture: Numbers (16) (17)
In today's reading, we see Aaron appeal for God's mercy as he stands between the living and the dead. Aaron risks his life by doing this to stop the plague. As you read this today, consider how this shows us a picture of Jesus and how He intervened for us on the cross!

Prayer
What is God saying to you? What do you need to say to God? Use a prayer model and your monthly prayer targets and requests as a guide.

DAY 62

Worship
Get alone with God. Find a quiet place. Sit down. Silence all distractions.

Scripture: Numbers (18) (19) (20)
As you read today, notice how consistent God's character is. We have seen over and over again His people disobey Him. While God gives them the consequences they deserve, he doesn't banish them from His family, He still shows them mercy.

Prayer
What is God saying to you? What do you need to say to God? Use a prayer model and your monthly prayer targets and requests as a guide.

DAY 63

Worship
Get alone with God. Find a quiet place. Sit down. Silence all distractions.

Scripture: Numbers ㉑ ㉒
In today's reading, we see God instruct Moses to craft a serpent on a pole for the people to look at and live if they are bitten by snakes sent to kill them. While it may seem like He asked Moses to create an idol for the people, notice that it actually points back to God's provision and rescue. The people are to turn to the serpent to be spared a physical death, just like we turn to Jesus to be saved from a spiritual death.

Prayer
What is God saying to you? What do you need to say to God? Use a prayer model and your monthly prayer targets and requests as a guide.

COMMUNITY

I attended a church service this week (circle):   YES   NO

I shared my faith and talked about my church with others this week (circle):   YES   NO

I connected with other Christians in a smaller group this week.
If yes, describe.

DAY 64

Worship
Get alone with God. Find a quiet place. Sit down. Silence all distractions.

Scripture: Numbers (23) (24) (25)
Today, we read about King Balak's attempt to curse the Israelites by hiring a prophet, Balaam, to curse them. His efforts are in vain as over and over again, Balaam's words come out as blessings instead of curses, until eventually comes a curse, but the curse is for King Balak rather than the Israelites. The blessings spoken by Balaam show Goes love for His people. They most certainly haven't been perfect, but He speaks highly of them through Balaam. Even when we've sinned, He sees our redemption!

Prayer
What is God saying to you? What do you need to say to God? Use a prayer model and your monthly prayer targets and requests as a guide.

DAY 65

Worship
Get alone with God. Find a quiet place. Sit down. Silence all distractions.

Scripture: Numbers (26) (27)
In today's reading, we see Zelophehad's five daughters, who had no sons, make their request to inherit the land that would have been given a son. Not only does God grant their request, but He makes it a new law. God is reasonable and generous and shows us the balance between His practical and emotional side.

Prayer
What is God saying to you? What do you need to say to God? Use a prayer model and your monthly prayer targets and requests as a guide.

DAY 66

Worship
Get alone with God. Find a quiet place. Sit down. Silence all distractions.

Scripture: Numbers (28) (29) (30)
In today's reading, we see God repeat a commandment that He's mentioned a few times before! Remember, when we see something repeated it typically means it's something important God needs us to understand. God is reminding us to rest! The Sabbath is about more than just relaxing and doing nothing; it's a day for us to reconnect with him.

Prayer
What is God saying to you? What do you need to say to God? Use a prayer model and your monthly prayer targets and requests as a guide.

DAY 67

Worship
Get alone with God. Find a quiet place. Sit down. Silence all distractions.

Scripture: Numbers (31) (32)
In today's reading, we see Moses order the death of the Midianite women, the same ones who tempted the Israelite men to go astray a few days ago. Moses is making sure he removes any temptation for sin by doing so. As you read today, think about how important it is for us to take control of our sinful nature and the things that tempt us. God knows we won't be perfect, but He wants us to find our joy in Him.

Prayer
What is God saying to you? What do you need to say to God? Use a prayer model and your monthly prayer targets and requests as a guide.

DAY 68

Worship
Get alone with God. Find a quiet place. Sit down. Silence all distractions.

Scripture: Numbers ㉝ ㉞
In Numbers 33:3-4, it says, "On their gods also the Lord executed judgments. We often think there are no other gods, but this verse in today's reading clarifies that God is superior to all other gods. Other gods may exist, but they are not equal to nor a threat to God!

Prayer
What is God saying to you? What do you need to say to God? Use a prayer model and your monthly prayer targets and requests as a guide.

DAY 69

Worship
Get alone with God. Find a quiet place. Sit down. Silence all distractions.

Scripture: Numbers ㉟ ㊱
Today's reading begins with recounting Israel's journey. As we end the book of Numbers, take a few extra moments to reflect on all you have read and learned about God so far.

Prayer
What is God saying to you? What do you need to say to God? Use a prayer model and your monthly prayer targets and requests as a guide.

DAY 70

Worship

Get alone with God. Find a quiet place. Sit down. Silence all distractions.

Scripture: Deuteronomy (1)(2)

Today we begin the book of Deuteronomy. Much of this book will feel like a refresher of everything we have read so far. Lean in as Moses gives us a recap; you may see something you didn't before!

Prayer

What is God saying to you? What do you need to say to God? Use a prayer model and your monthly prayer targets and requests as a guide.

COMMUNITY

I attended a church service this week (circle):   YES   NO

I shared my faith and talked about my church with others this week (circle):   YES   NO

I connected with other Christians in a smaller group this week.
If yes, describe.

DAY 71

Worship
Get alone with God. Find a quiet place. Sit down. Silence all distractions.

Scripture: Deuteronomy (3)(4)
In today's reading, we see God give Moses one of his final roles as a leader-to train and encourage Joseph since he will be the one leading the people into the promised land. Moses faithfully sets aside his own desires to do so. He fully trusts God and His plan, which serves as a great reminder that we can trust God with our lives, even when it's difficult.

Prayer
What is God saying to you? What do you need to say to God? Use a prayer model and your monthly prayer targets and requests as a guide.

DAY 72

Worship
Get alone with God. Find a quiet place. Sit down. Silence all distractions.

Scripture: Deuteronomy (5)(6)(7)
As you read today, take a moment to recount God's faithfulness. Everything you have, you can attribute to Him, just like the Israelites. He didn't choose them because of who they were; He grew them through relationship with Him!

Prayer
What is God saying to you? What do you need to say to God? Use a prayer model and your monthly prayer targets and requests as a guide.

DAY 73

Worship
Get alone with God. Find a quiet place. Sit down. Silence all distractions.

Scripture: Deuteronomy ⑧ ⑨ ⑩
Today, in Deuteronomy 10:14-15, we read, "Behold, to the Lord your God belong heaven and the heaven of heavens, the earth with all that is in it. Yet the Lord set his heart in love on your fathers and chose their offspring after them, you above all peoples, as you are this day." Everything belongs to God; he lacks for nothing, but the one thing he wants is a relationship with us.

Prayer
What is God saying to you? What do you need to say to God? Use a prayer model and your monthly prayer targets and requests as a guide.

DAY 74

Worship
Get alone with God. Find a quiet place. Sit down. Silence all distractions.

Scripture: Deuteronomy ⑪ ⑫ ⑬
Today's reading opens with God giving a command to love Him. This may seem odd, to command love, but God then reminds them of all He brought them through. God is our provider and protector, and in return, He wants our love and obedience!

Prayer
What is God saying to you? What do you need to say to God? Use a prayer model and your monthly prayer targets and requests as a guide.

DAY 75

Worship
Get alone with God. Find a quiet place. Sit down. Silence all distractions.

Scripture: Deuteronomy ⑭ ⑮ ⑯
In today's reading we see Moses giving more laws from God. It can be tempting to skim the pages and not fully process what you are reading but lean in and think about how God wants to protect our hearts, and how many laws are in place to do just that, to protect us and keep us not only obedient but truly connected to Him.

Prayer
What is God saying to you? What do you need to say to God? Use a prayer model and your monthly prayer targets and requests as a guide.

DAY 76

Worship
Get alone with God. Find a quiet place. Sit down. Silence all distractions.

Scripture: Deuteronomy ⑰ ⑱ ⑲ ⑳
Keep an open mind as you read today. We read about more laws that Moses is giving to the people as he is preparing them for a time when they will no longer be wandering in the desert. Pray and ask God to give you eyes to see and wisdom to understand!

Prayer
What is God saying to you? What do you need to say to God? Use a prayer model and your monthly prayer targets and requests as a guide.

DAY 77

Worship
Get alone with God. Find a quiet place. Sit down. Silence all distractions.

Scripture: Deuteronomy ㉑ ㉒ ㉓
Be encouraged as you read today's passages. Moses continues his speech and is giving a variety of laws to the Israelites. While some of the laws may be potentially confusing, remember that God has a heart for justice and protecting his people.

Prayer
What is God saying to you? What do you need to say to God? Use a prayer model and your monthly prayer targets and requests as a guide.

COMMUNITY

I attended a church service this week (circle):   YES   NO

I shared my faith and talked about my church with others this week (circle):   YES   NO

I connected with other Christians in a smaller group this week.
If yes, describe.

DAY 78

Worship

Get alone with God. Find a quiet place. Sit down. Silence all distractions.

Scripture: Deuteronomy (24) (25) (26) (27)

You'll notice in today's reading that God is very possessive and protective of His people. Not one specific class of people either. He cares for everyone. He is no respecter of man and status. All He cares about is letting His creation know how much He loves them. While reading, pay attention to how God cares for His people.

Prayer

What is God saying to you? What do you need to say to God? Use a prayer model and your monthly prayer targets and requests as a guide.

DAY 79

Worship

Get alone with God. Find a quiet place. Sit down. Silence all distractions.

Scripture: Deuteronomy (28) (29)

In today's reading, watch for God's intentionality to detail. There's a reason behind everything He does and how He communicates His promises to the Israelites. Think about how God speaks to you and fulfills promises in your life. If there's one thing that is a common theme, He blesses generously.

Prayer

What is God saying to you? What do you need to say to God? Use a prayer model and your monthly prayer targets and requests as a guide.

DAY 80

Worship
Get alone with God. Find a quiet place. Sit down. Silence all distractions.

Scripture: Deuteronomy 30 31
You'll see there's simplicity in how God builds and connects with us. He's not surprised by our sin, and He's definitely not surprised by our stubborn attitudes to repent. He is love in a way we can't understand on this side of eternity, but as you read, pay attention to how Moses directs the Israelites back to God.

Prayer
What is God saying to you? What do you need to say to God? Use a prayer model and your monthly prayer targets and requests as a guide.

DAY 81

Worship
Get alone with God. Find a quiet place. Sit down. Silence all distractions.

Scripture: Deuteronomy 32 33 34   Psalm 91
Today, we finish reading the Torah! As you dive in today, you'll notice something. Not just in the reading, but in your own heart. You're on your 81st day, and without a doubt, your heart is drawing closer and closer to God. So as you read, keep that in mind because it ties into it.

Prayer
What is God saying to you? What do you need to say to God? Use a prayer model and your monthly prayer targets and requests as a guide.

DAY 82

Worship

Get alone with God. Find a quiet place. Sit down. Silence all distractions.

Scripture: Joshua (1) (2) (3) (4)

Today we begin reading the first of the history books, Joshua. While this book will provide historical information, remember that it will also reveal the character of God and keep seeking Him as you read!

Prayer

What is God saying to you? What do you need to say to God? Use a prayer model and your monthly prayer targets and requests as a guide.

DAY 83

Worship

Get alone with God. Find a quiet place. Sit down. Silence all distractions.

Scripture: Joshua (5) (6) (7) (8)

Today, we read about the Battle of Jericho. As you read, consider how the Israelites may have felt as they began circling the walls of Jericho. There may have been moments where they wondered if they were wasting their time, but even in the moments of waiting, God is at work!

Prayer

What is God saying to you? What do you need to say to God? Use a prayer model and your monthly prayer targets and requests as a guide.

DAY 84

Worship
Get alone with God. Find a quiet place. Sit down. Silence all distractions.

Scripture: Joshua ⑨ ⑩ ⑪
As you read today, notice how even though Joshua was faithful and obedient to God, victory wasn't immediate. God doesn't always give us the easy way out, but He's always working on our behalf!

Prayer
What is God saying to you? What do you need to say to God? Use a prayer model and your monthly prayer targets and requests as a guide.

COMMUNITY

I attended a church service this week (circle):   YES   NO

I shared my faith and talked about my church with others this week (circle):   YES   NO

I connected with other Christians in a smaller group this week.
If yes, describe.

DAY 85

Worship
Get alone with God. Find a quiet place. Sit down. Silence all distractions.

Scripture: Joshua (12) (13) (14) (15)
As you ready today, reflect on a time when you've not been successful in something you were called to do. When we experience delays and failures, God is still shaping our hearts. He may not always change our experiences, but those experiences can change our perspective if we lean into Him.

Prayer
What is God saying to you? What do you need to say to God? Use a prayer model and your monthly prayer targets and requests as a guide.

DAY 86

Worship
Get alone with God. Find a quiet place. Sit down. Silence all distractions.

Scripture: Joshua (16) (17) (18)
Today we read about the allotments of land being split amongst the tribes. They've been waiting a long time for this and are likely getting antsy. God repeatedly told them to drive out the Canaanites, but most tribes are more worried about what land they will receive than they are about obeying God's orders. How often do we do this? Many times, we feel stuck in the same spot because we haven't been obedient to the last thing God told us to do. We see progress when we take steps that God gives us, one by one, even when the process feels long.

Prayer
What is God saying to you? What do you need to say to God? Use a prayer model and your monthly prayer targets and requests as a guide.

DAY 87

Worship
Get alone with God. Find a quiet place. Sit down. Silence all distractions.

Scripture: Joshua (19) (20) (21)
Today, we read more about the division of land for the Israelites. We see God's character as we reflect on the journey of the Israelites. He has been generous and faithful, forgiving and merciful despite all of the times His people wandered from Him. He gives us everything we need, even when we don't deserve it!

Prayer
What is God saying to you? What do you need to say to God? Use a prayer model and your monthly prayer targets and requests as a guide.t

DAY 88

Worship
Get alone with God. Find a quiet place. Sit down. Silence all distractions.

Scriptures: Joshua (22) (23) (24)
Joshua 23:14 says "You know in your hearts and souls, all of you, that not one word has failed of all the good things that the Lord your God promised concerning you. All have come to pass for you; not one of them has failed." We see the Israelites beginning to walk in the promises from God. They're in the promised land, they've become a great nation, and most importantly, they are living in relationship with Him!

Prayer
What is God saying to you? What do you need to say to God? Use a prayer model and your monthly prayer targets and requests as a guide.

DAY 89

Worship
Get alone with God. Find a quiet place. Sit down. Silence all distractions.

Scripture: Judges (1)(2)
Today we begin reading the book of Judges. The term "Judges" in this book refers to civil and military leaders who enact laws and command the army. The Canaanites are still living on the land that the Israelites now own because they haven't been obedient and driven them out like God commanded. God knew this would cause problems for the Israelites. Like any good parent, He tried to protect the Israelites from doing things the hard way. We see how much God loves His people as he disciplines them for their disobedience.

Prayer
What is God saying to you? What do you need to say to God? Use a prayer model and your monthly prayer targets and requests as a guide.

DAY 90

Worship
Get alone with God. Find a quiet place. Sit down. Silence all distractions.

Scripture: Judges (3)(4)(5)
In today's reading, we see the first four judges that were appointed by God. These seem to be unlikely leaders, including a Canaanite and a woman. But God sees potential in these leaders and reveals Himself at work as He works through those who might otherwise be overlooked!

Prayer
What is God saying to you? What do you need to say to God? Use a prayer model and your monthly prayer targets and requests as a guide.

DAY 91

Worship
Get alone with God. Find a quiet place. Sit down. Silence all distractions.

Scripture: Judges ⑥ ⑦
Today we meet a man named Gideon whom God appoints to deliver Israel from oppression. Just like the Judges we read about yesterday, Gideon is an unlikely leader. He doubts that he can do what God is asking him to do. He also doubts God, but God comes alongside Gideon and, He is with Gideon just like He is with us.

Prayer
What is God saying to you? What do you need to say to God? Use a prayer model and your monthly prayer targets and requests as a guide.

COMMUNITY

I attended a church service this week (circle):   YES   NO

I shared my faith and talked about my church with others this week (circle):   YES   NO

I connected with other Christians in a smaller group this week. If yes, describe.

DAY 92

Worship
Get alone with God. Find a quiet place. Sit down. Silence all distractions.

Scripture: Judges (8)(9)
Today, we read about Gideon's son, Abimelech, who kills his own brothers because of his own selfish desires. We see God's heart for justice when he intervenes. Anytime something or someone threatens the people that He loves, we see the wrath of God. Remember, just like a parent whose child is in danger, God wants to protect and defend us.

Prayer
What is God saying to you? What do you need to say to God? Use a prayer model and your monthly prayer targets and requests as a guide.

DAY 93

Worship
Get alone with God. Find a quiet place. Sit down. Silence all distractions.

Scripture: Judges (10)(11)(12)
In today's reading, we see the Israelites continue to disobey God and worship other gods. Judges 10:16 says, "He became patient over the misery of Israel." His people continue to disappoint and rebel against Him, and he punishes them, but all the while, His heart is aching because of the misery they are causing themselves. God grieves with us, even when our pain is self-inflicted.

Prayer
What is God saying to you? What do you need to say to God? Use a prayer model and your monthly prayer targets and requests as a guide.

DAY 94

Worship
Get alone with God. Find a quiet place. Sit down. Silence all distractions.

Scripture: Judges (13) (14) (15)
Today, we read about Samson, a wicked judge. God uses Samson to accomplish His plan. While this may be confusing, sometimes God uses wicked people to defeat a greater enemy. God can do anything, and He uses us despite ourselves.

Prayer
What is God saying to you? What do you need to say to God? Use a prayer model and your monthly prayer targets and requests as a guide.

DAY 95

Worship
Get alone with God. Find a quiet place. Sit down. Silence all distractions.

Scripture: Judges (16) (17) (18)
In today's reading, we see Samson in a moment of weakness and vulnerability. It's in this moment that he cries out to God and asks for strength, and God shows up. God wants intimacy with us, even when we least deserve Him.

Prayer
What is God saying to you? What do you need to say to God? Use a prayer model and your monthly prayer targets and requests as a guide.

DAY 96

Worship
Get alone with God. Find a quiet place. Sit down. Silence all distractions.

Scripture: Judges ⑲ ⑳ ㉑
Today's reading has some elements that may be difficult to process. Remember as you read that just because it's in the Bible does not mean it is endorsed by God. Some parts of the Bible are descriptive, telling us what happened, not telling us what we should do or what is right.

Prayer
What is God saying to you? What do you need to say to God? Use a prayer model and your monthly prayer targets and requests as a guide.

DAY 97

Worship
Get alone with God. Find a quiet place. Sit down. Silence all distractions.

Scripture: Ruth ① ② ③ ④
Today, we read the book of Ruth. This is a great transition after reading the book of Judges! We see in this book God's heart for redemption. Ruth is a widow who commits to family and follows her mother-in-law back to her home in Israel, and as a result, is in the genealogy of Jesus

Prayer
What is God saying to you? What do you need to say to God? Use a prayer model and your monthly prayer targets and requests as a guide.

DAY 98

Worship
Get alone with God. Find a quiet place. Sit down. Silence all distractions.

Scripture: 1 Samuel (1) (2) (3)
We start the book of 1 Samuel today; it has been decades since the Israelites have heard from God. We meet Hannah, the only female recorded in scripture who went to the tabernacle. Hannah is barren and cries to God; she takes her pain directly to Him. Hannah knew that God could be trusted, even though she didn't know what the outcome would be. As you read today, remember that God wants intimacy with us, and he can be trusted with our hearts.

Prayer
What is God saying to you? What do you need to say to God? Use a prayer model and your monthly prayer targets and requests as a guide.

COMMUNITY

I attended a church service this week (circle):   YES   NO

I shared my faith and talked about my church with others this week (circle):   YES   NO

I connected with other Christians in a smaller group this week.
If yes, describe.

DAY 99

Worship

Get alone with God. Find a quiet place. Sit down. Silence all distractions.

Scripture: 1 Samuel ④ ⑤ ⑥ ⑦ ⑧

Notice today how even though the Israelites are God's chosen people, they are driven by fear of man rather than the love of God. How often do you place the opinions and acceptance of man over your relationship with Him?

Prayer

What is God saying to you? What do you need to say to God? Use a prayer model and your monthly prayer targets and requests as a guide.

DAY 100

Worship

Get alone with God. Find a quiet place. Sit down. Silence all distractions.

Scripture: 1 Samuel ⑨ ⑩ ⑪ ⑫

You've reached day 100! Take a moment to reflect on what you've read and learned about God's character so far. How has reading God's word for the past 100 days changed you and your walk with Him?

Prayer

What is God saying to you? What do you need to say to God? Use a prayer model and your monthly prayer targets and requests as a guide.

DAY 101

Worship
Get alone with God. Find a quiet place. Sit down. Silence all distractions.

Scripture: 1 Samuel (13) (14)
In today's reading, we see a time when Israel's King, Saul, disregards God's commands and in a time of pressure and fear, acts on His own, outside of the will of God. In contrast, his son, Jonathan, acts in faith and courage. As you read, think about what made Saul and Jonathan different.

Prayer
What is God saying to you? What do you need to say to God? Use a prayer model and your monthly prayer targets and requests as a guide.

DAY 102

Worship
Get alone with God. Find a quiet place. Sit down. Silence all distractions.

Scripture: 1 Samuel (15) (16) (17)
As you read today's passage, focus on the difference between Saul and the shepherd David. How was David different, and how did Saul respond to David's success?

Prayer
What is God saying to you? What do you need to say to God? Use a prayer model and your monthly prayer targets and requests as a guide.

DAY 103

Worship

Get alone with God. Find a quiet place. Sit down. Silence all distractions.

Scripture: 1 Samuel (18) (19) (20)   Psalm (11) (59)

What happens when we are motivated by fear and insecurity? Notice today how even when others plan to harm us, God always protects those who honor and trust him.

Prayer

What is God saying to you? What do you need to say to God? Use a prayer model and your monthly prayer targets and requests as a guide.

DAY 104

Worship

Get alone with God. Find a quiet place. Sit down. Silence all distractions.

Scripture: 1 Samuel (21) (22) (23) (24)

Today focus on the goodness of God even when all our circumstances seem to work against us. Notice how God always thwarts the schemes of our enemies in our favor. Notice how David continues to honor Saul even when He is acting against him and God.

Prayer

What is God saying to you? What do you need to say to God? Use a prayer model and your monthly prayer targets and requests as a guide.

DAY 105

Worship
Get alone with God. Find a quiet place. Sit down. Silence all distractions.

Scripture: Psalm (7) (27) (31) (32) (52)
Notice how David relates to God. David desired closeness to God more than anything else, even comfort in life. David bookends his laments with praise to God. He refers to God as a stronghold and refuge.

Prayer
What is God saying to you? What do you need to say to God? Use a prayer model and your monthly prayer targets and requests as a guide.

COMMUNITY

I attended a church service this week (circle):   YES   NO

I shared my faith and talked about my church with others this week (circle):   YES   NO

I connected with other Christians in a smaller group this week.
If yes, describe.

DAY 106

Worship
Get alone with God. Find a quiet place. Sit down. Silence all distractions.

Scripture: Psalm (56) (120) (140) (141) (142)
Focus on relating to David today. David, repeatedly in trouble, acknowledges that God is with Him and is not distant. God is with us even when we don't feel it. David was honest and unpolished in his thoughts and prayers.

Prayer
What is God saying to you? What do you need to say to God? Use a prayer model and your monthly prayer targets and requests as a guide.

DAY 107

Worship
Get alone with God. Find a quiet place. Sit down. Silence all distractions.

Scripture: 1 Samuel (25) (26) (27)
How many times in our anger do we strike out at others? We want justice, but did you know that God wants justice even more. Today we see David trusting that God will deliver justice even when David wants to take matters into his own hands. David yielded to God, not to his desires.

Prayer
What is God saying to you? What do you need to say to God? Use a prayer model and your monthly prayer targets and requests as a guide.

DAY 108

Worship
Get alone with God. Find a quiet place. Sit down. Silence all distractions.

Scripture: Psalm (17) (35) (54) (63)
Have you ever felt accused or that life is unfair? God sees who we are when no one is looking and He will reward us eternally. True fulfillment is only in our relationship with God. In His isolation, David longs to be able to worship God in the Temple and the Feasts. Even though He is far from the Temple, he isn't far from God. How can we rejoice in God regardless of our circumstances?

Prayer
What is God saying to you? What do you need to say to God? Use a prayer model and your monthly prayer targets and requests as a guide.

DAY 109

Worship
Get alone with God. Find a quiet place. Sit down. Silence all distractions.

Scripture: 1 Samuel (28) (29) (30) (31)   Psalm (18)
Today you've finished your 10th book of the Bible. How has reading God's word changed you? Focus on what you've learned about who God is, His character. Why do you think God doesn't speak or answer King Saul?

Prayer
What is God saying to you? What do you need to say to God? Use a prayer model and your monthly prayer targets and requests as a guide.

DAY 110

Worship

Get alone with God. Find a quiet place. Sit down. Silence all distractions.

Scripture: Psalm (121) (123) (124) (125) (128) (129) (130)

Focus on who God is and what He has done for you today. Take some time to pause and really focus on the goodness of God. Sometimes it can be easy to forget the good things that God has given us. How has God blessed you in the past, and what are you believing God for in the future?

Prayer

What is God saying to you? What do you need to say to God? Use a prayer model and your monthly prayer targets and requests as a guide.

DAY 111

Worship

Get alone with God. Find a quiet place. Sit down. Silence all distractions.

Scripture: 2 Samuel (1) (2) (3) (4)

Notice today how David consults God first and how much he honors God and the authority God has set up. He mourns the death of Saul and Jonathan. God continues to bless him in the midst of uncertainty.

Prayer

What is God saying to you? What do you need to say to God? Use a prayer model and your monthly prayer targets and requests as a guide.

DAY 112

Worship
Get alone with God. Find a quiet place. Sit down. Silence all distractions.

Scripture: Psalm (6)(8)(9)(10)(14)(16)(19)(21)
David wrote about one half of the book of Psalms. David regularly wrote in poetic language and was honest about how he felt in any given situation. While he expressed his feelings, he always comes back to the sovereignty and goodness of God.

Prayer
What is God saying to you? What do you need to say to God? Use a prayer model and your monthly prayer targets and requests as a guide.

COMMUNITY

I attended a church service this week (circle):   YES   NO

I shared my faith and talked about my church with others this week (circle):   YES   NO

I connected with other Christians in a smaller group this week.
If yes, describe.

DAY 113

Worship
Get alone with God. Find a quiet place. Sit down. Silence all distractions.

Scripture: 1 Chronicles (1)(2)
How do we respond when we experience the consequences of our actions? Do we blame God, or do we honestly assess our role in what happened? God is good, and His ways are perfect. God uses everything in His plan, even those things that cause pain and suffering to His people.

Prayer
What is God saying to you? What do you need to say to God? Use a prayer model and your monthly prayer targets and requests as a guide.

DAY 114

Worship
Get alone with God. Find a quiet place. Sit down. Silence all distractions.

Scripture: Psalm (43)(44)(45)(49)(84)(85)(87)
Again, David continues to encourage himself. David is very honest with what he is feeling but always circles back to who God is, not just in his life but in the life of his ancestors. He asserts that it is God who brings victory, not the deeds of men.

Prayer
What is God saying to you? What do you need to say to God? Use a prayer model and your monthly prayer targets and requests as a guide.

DAY 115

Worship
Get alone with God. Find a quiet place. Sit down. Silence all distractions.

Scripture: 1 Chronicles ③ ④ ⑤
Today, we see how important it is to ask God for his protection and his blessing. God openly listens to all kinds of prayers. God cares that we bring to him the things that are on our minds and in our hearts. God sifts our prayers and makes sure to answer those that benefit and bless us.

Prayer
What is God saying to you? What do you need to say to God? Use a prayer model and your monthly prayer targets and requests as a guide.

DAY 116

Worship
Get alone with God. Find a quiet place. Sit down. Silence all distractions.

Scripture: Psalm ⑦③ ⑦⑦ ⑦⑧
As you consider what is most important in life, consider that this life is not all there is. Sometimes we can get tunnel vision on all this life has to offer, but what about eternal life? Many times we need to take our minds off of what this world values and center it on God.

Prayer
What is God saying to you? What do you need to say to God? Use a prayer model and your monthly prayer targets and requests as a guide.

DAY 117

Worship

Get alone with God. Find a quiet place. Sit down. Silence all distractions.

Scripture: 1 Chronicles (6)

Genealogies are so important in the Bible. They determine a lot. Notice the cities of refuge mentioned. What do they say about the grace and mercy of God?

Prayer

What is God saying to you? What do you need to say to God? Use a prayer model and your monthly prayer targets and requests as a guide.

DAY 118

Worship

Get alone with God. Find a quiet place. Sit down. Silence all distractions.

Scripture: Psalm (81) (88) (92) (93)

Focus on the words "Hear" and "Listen" today. So many times, we get into trouble when we don't apply God's instruction to our lives. Again in the Psalms, we see that God wants to hear what is in our hearts, even when it is less than pleasant. Focus on those things that are temporal and eternal.

Prayer

What is God saying to you? What do you need to say to God? Use a prayer model and your monthly prayer targets and requests as a guide.

DAY 119

Worship

Get alone with God. Find a quiet place. Sit down. Silence all distractions.

Scripture: 1 Chronicles (7)(8)(9)(10)

What is God teaching us about himself? Notice the leader of God's people didn't seek God. God is the giver and taker of life. God is protective and defends His children. He is vigilant when eternity is at stake.

Prayer

What is God saying to you? What do you need to say to God? Use a prayer model and your monthly prayer targets and requests as a guide.

COMMUNITY

I attended a church service this week (circle):   YES   NO

I shared my faith and talked about my church with others this week (circle):   YES   NO

I connected with other Christians in a smaller group this week.
If yes, describe.

DAY 120

Worship
Get alone with God. Find a quiet place. Sit down. Silence all distractions.

Scripture: Psalm (102) (103) (104)
What do you do when you feel alone and distressed? By remembering that God is the God of rescue, it helps us push through the moments when we are suffering, either from the consequences of someone else's sin or our own sin. By remembering who God is, gracious and merciful, we can take comfort in and look forward to eternity.

Prayer
What is God saying to you? What do you need to say to God? Use a prayer model and your monthly prayer targets and requests as a guide.

DAY 121

Worship
Get alone with God. Find a quiet place. Sit down. Silence all distractions.

Scripture: 2 Samuel (5)   1 Chronicles (11) (12)
David becomes King over all of Israel. Remember, he was anointed King of Israel by the Prophet Samuel, but it took almost twenty years for him to finally become the King. Today, think about a time when things didn't happen as fast as you thought. How did waiting help prepare you for the future?

Prayer
What is God saying to you? What do you need to say to God? Use a prayer model and your monthly prayer targets and requests as a guide.

DAY 122

Worship
Get alone with God. Find a quiet place. Sit down. Silence all distractions.

Scripture: Psalm (133)
Today you are one-third of the way through the entire Bible! Today is a Psalm about praise and worship. Focus on the goodness of God to you in the past. Then allow it to move you forward towards His plans for your future. God's way is the best way, and His plan for you is good. God always keeps his promises.

Prayer
What is God saying to you? What do you need to say to God? Use a prayer model and your monthly prayer targets and requests as a guide.

DAY 123

Worship
Get alone with God. Find a quiet place. Sit down. Silence all distractions.

Scripture: Psalm (106) (107)
Focus on unity. Not just personally but together with God's people. How does God respond when we are unfaithful? What can you learn about who God is and what his motives are? What are the consequences when we abandon God? What is God's response? How does He respond to our time of need?

Prayer
What is God saying to you? What do you need to say to God? Use a prayer model and your monthly prayer targets and requests as a guide.

DAY 124

Worship

Get alone with God. Find a quiet place. Sit down. Silence all distractions.

Scripture: 1 Chronicles (13) (14) (15) (16)

How does disobedience to God cause us harm? God is holy, but we aren't, and he has given us rules to be close to him. He may give us mercy, but it is His alone to give. God can invoke a response from not only his children but also His enemies. How can you relate to David?

Prayer

What is God saying to you? What do you need to say to God? Use a prayer model and your monthly prayer targets and requests as a guide.

DAY 125

Worship

Get alone with God. Find a quiet place. Sit down. Silence all distractions.

Scripture: Psalm (1) (2) (15) (22) (23) (24) (47) (68)

What is the difference between a wicked man and a righteous man? God laughs at His enemies because He is just, and there is no way a wicked person can succeed. God is holy and we are not, even on our best days, he is better. Focus today on God's holiness.

Prayer

What is God saying to you? What do you need to say to God? Use a prayer model and your monthly prayer targets and requests as a guide.

DAY 126

Worship
Get alone with God. Find a quiet place. Sit down. Silence all distractions.

Scripture: Psalm (89) (96) (100) (101) (105) (132)
Even when evil things happen and evil people seem to win, God is still good and works all things to His purposes. Even though we are sinful, God invites us into his presence. How does being in God's presence change the intentions of our hearts?

Prayer
What is God saying to you? What do you need to say to God? Use a prayer model and your monthly prayer targets and requests as a guide.

COMMUNITY

I attended a church service this week (circle):   YES   NO

I shared my faith and talked about my church with others this week (circle):   YES   NO

I connected with other Christians in a smaller group this week.
If yes, describe.

DAY 127

Worship

Get alone with God. Find a quiet place. Sit down. Silence all distractions.

Scripture: 2 Samuel (6)(7)　1 Chronicles (17)

Proper fear of God is made up of delight and awe, whereas an improper fear of God drives you away from God. Focus today on David's desire here to please God by building Him a temple and how God says no. Consider how even when God says no, it isn't to hold us back or hurt us but to help us and set us up for His future for us.

Prayer

What is God saying to you? What do you need to say to God? Use a prayer model and your monthly prayer targets and requests as a guide.

DAY 128

Worship

Get alone with God. Find a quiet place. Sit down. Silence all distractions.

Scripture: Psalm (25) (29) (33) (36) (39)

Notice the wide variety of emotions in today's reading. David is honest and humble about what He knows about himself and appeals to God's goodness and friendship. When we fail to praise God, we are acting against God's purpose. Even in our sin, because we are righteous and not given over to sin, we can appeal to God's forgiveness for renewal.

Prayer

What is God saying to you? What do you need to say to God? Use a prayer model and your monthly prayer targets and requests as a guide.

DAY 129

Worship

Get alone with God. Find a quiet place. Sit down. Silence all distractions.

Scripture: 2 Samuel (8) (9)   1 Chronicles (18)

Notice how God was working to fulfill his Covenant with David. It is not David that gains victory from his strength or ability, but God is the one who grants victory, not David. David offers the spoils of his victories to God, and in the future, those spoils are used to make the articles in the Temple built by David's son, Solomon.

Prayer

What is God saying to you? What do you need to say to God? Use a prayer model and your monthly prayer targets and requests as a guide.

DAY 130

Worship

Get alone with God. Find a quiet place. Sit down. Silence all distractions.

Scripture: Psalm (50) (53) (60) (75)

The sacrificial system was not a way to make right what the people did wrong but instead a way for the people to align their hearts with God. Surrender is the path to freedom. We need to humble ourselves before the holiness and goodness of God.

Prayer

What is God saying to you? What do you need to say to God? Use a prayer model and your monthly prayer targets and requests as a guide.

DAY 131

Worship

Get alone with God. Find a quiet place. Sit down. Silence all distractions.

Scripture: 2 Samuel (10)   1 Chronicles (19)   Psalm (20)

David didn't have to keep the peace, but He desired peace for the good of all. God is trustworthy, and notice that even in the face of war, God gives victory to Israel. Look for God's love and care for all people in today's reading.

Prayer

What is God saying to you? What do you need to say to God? Use a prayer model and your monthly prayer targets and requests as a guide.

DAY 132

Worship

Get alone with God. Find a quiet place. Sit down. Silence all distractions.

Scripture: Psalm (65) (66) (67) (69) (70)

How can you turn your heart to praise today? Even in moments where we are weak and can't rescue ourselves, God comes through for us not just by meeting our needs but by giving us more than we need. David has a God-honoring view of his life, the good and the bad. In all, notice that God is good and can be trusted.

Prayer

What is God saying to you? What do you need to say to God? Use a prayer model and your monthly prayer targets and requests as a guide.

DAY 133

Worship
Get alone with God. Find a quiet place. Sit down. Silence all distractions.

Scripture: 2 Samuel (11)(12)   1 Chronicles (20)
Today we see David not where he was supposed to be. Instead, he put himself in a compromising position that leads to much pain and suffering for him and those he leads. David fails here by sleeping with another man's wife. When confronted by the prophet, David repents of his sin and God gives mercy to David. You see David's true repentance following the consequences of David's actions, not by avoiding them.

Prayer
What is God saying to you? What do you need to say to God? Use a prayer model and your monthly prayer targets and requests as a guide.

COMMUNITY

I attended a church service this week (circle):   YES   NO

I shared my faith and talked about my church with others this week (circle):   YES   NO

I connected with other Christians in a smaller group this week. If yes, describe.

DAY 134

Scripture: Psalm (32) (51) (86) (122)
Notice here how God still blesses us even when we sin. God doesn't bless our sins but gives us mercy. God covers our sin so that we can still have a relationship with Him. This is the power of the Gospel and how Jesus dies on the cross to forgive our sins past, present, and future. Why? So that we can overcome sin and have relationship with God. We need to go to God when we sin, not run from God.

DAY 135

Scripture: 2 Samuel (13) (14) (15)
Even when we repent and turn to God, the consequences of our sins affect those around us. Lust is impatient, selfish, and without reason, in contrast to the love of God. We see the sins of David visited on his children. This results in David having to flee from Jerusalem because of his son attempting to overthrow the kingdom. In the end, God's timing is perfect, and once again, God keeps His promise by defending and establishing David.

DAY 136

Worship
Get alone with God. Find a quiet place. Sit down. Silence all distractions.

Scripture: Psalm ③ ④ ⑫ ⑬ ㉘ ㊺
God doesn't just want to hear our praise, but He also wants to hear our heart, even at our low points. It isn't that we have those feelings but that we allow God to process us in light of His goodness and sovereignty. Our peace is found in the nearness of God, not in our circumstances.

Prayer
What is God saying to you? What do you need to say to God? Use a prayer model and your monthly prayer targets and requests as a guide.

DAY 137

Worship
Get alone with God. Find a quiet place. Sit down. Silence all distractions.

Scripture: 2 Samuel ⑯ ⑰ ⑱
God's timing is perfect, even when we can't see the whole picture. David continues to humbly receive whatever happens and trust God and fights away his desire to retaliate. Notice today how the prophecy in 2 Samuel 12 is fulfilled. Even though David is still living out the consequences of previous sin, God is still faithful and still working things for his good.

Prayer
What is God saying to you? What do you need to say to God? Use a prayer model and your monthly prayer targets and requests as a guide.

DAY 138

Worship
Get alone with God. Find a quiet place. Sit down. Silence all distractions.

Scripture: Psalm (26) (40) (58) (61) (62) (64)
Notice today how David gives the credit to God. David is aware of his sin, and it humbles him before a perfect God. He has nothing to offer God. This is what true spiritual humility looks like. It is in this humility that God responds and works on our behalf. Notice how raw and honest David is.

Prayer
What is God saying to you? What do you need to say to God? Use a prayer model and your monthly prayer targets and requests as a guide.

DAY 139

Worship
Get alone with God. Find a quiet place. Sit down. Silence all distractions.

Scripture: 2 Samuel (19) (20) (21)
When we offer grace and forgiveness to others, we are most like God. Even when it would be justified to seek revenge, God calls David to make peace. David was a king that viewed himself as a servant, a servant of God. David wasn't perfect, but he wanted a united kingdom that honored God.

Prayer
What is God saying to you? What do you need to say to God? Use a prayer model and your monthly prayer targets and requests as a guide.

DAY 140

Worship
Get alone with God. Find a quiet place. Sit down. Silence all distractions.

Scripture: Psalm ⑤ ㊳ ㊶ ㊷
Even rulers of nations are still under God, and it is God who is in control. All goodness comes from God. David loves justice and God because God is just. Even when we are sinful, God wants to be near to us. Grace is when we get what we don't deserve, and mercy is when we don't get what we do deserve. Focus on the grace and mercy of God as you read.

Prayer
What is God saying to you? What do you need to say to God? Use a prayer model and your monthly prayer targets and requests as a guide.

COMMUNITY

I attended a church service this week (circle):   YES   NO

I shared my faith and talked about my church with others this week (circle):   YES   NO

I connected with other Christians in a smaller group this week. If yes, describe.

DAY 141

Worship

Get alone with God. Find a quiet place. Sit down. Silence all distractions.

Scripture: 2 Samuel ㉒ ㉓ Psalm (57)

How can you see the goodness of God to David? How does this help you see God's goodness in your life? Many times, we can only see clearly is in hindsight. Consider how faithful God has been to you when you've obeyed him and even when you've disobeyed him.

Prayer

What is God saying to you? What do you need to say to God? Use a prayer model and your monthly prayer targets and requests as a guide.

DAY 142

Worship

Get alone with God. Find a quiet place. Sit down. Silence all distractions.

Scripture: Psalm (95) (97) (98) (99)

God isn't just supreme over the earth but the heavens as well. Here we see three humble postures of worship. God is our maker and our shepherd. He is with us, watching over us as we continue to walk with him. A relationship with God brings rest and restoration. God also overcomes every obstacle we face.

Prayer

What is God saying to you? What do you need to say to God? Use a prayer model and your monthly prayer targets and requests as a guide.

DAY 143

Worship
Get alone with God. Find a quiet place. Sit down. Silence all distractions.

Scripture: 2 Samuel (24) 1 Chronicles (21) (22) Psalm (30)
God puts people in our lives to help us make good decisions. Today we see a time when David doesn't heed the advice of one of his most trusted friends. Instead, he doesn't consult God and moves forward with a nationwide census. It was the motivation of David's actions that made them sinful, and once again, consequences follow. Even in the consequences, we see the goodness of God to his servant David.

Prayer
What is God saying to you? What do you need to say to God? Use a prayer model and your monthly prayer targets and requests as a guide.

DAY 144

Worship
Get alone with God. Find a quiet place. Sit down. Silence all distractions.

Scripture: Psalm (108) (109) (110)
It is so important that we are honest to God but also appeal to God in spite of our feelings. God is a safe place as long as our heart is turned towards Him. Today look for Jesus in the reading. We can't save our self, and we need Jesus to save us and redeem us.

Prayer
What is God saying to you? What do you need to say to God? Use a prayer model and your monthly prayer targets and requests as a guide.

DAY 145

Worship
Get alone with God. Find a quiet place. Sit down. Silence all distractions.

Scripture: 1 Chronicles (23) (24) (25)
Consider the significance of the Temple and a permanent place for worship. Notice the details and those who are set apart for temple service. Imagine a time when something you loved that was temporary became permanent. God is establishing His people by providing a permanent place of worship, foreshadowing a time when He will dwell in us as Christians.

Prayer
What is God saying to you? What do you need to say to God? Use a prayer model and your monthly prayer targets and requests as a guide.

DAY 146

Worship
Get alone with God. Find a quiet place. Sit down. Silence all distractions.

Scripture: Psalm (131) (138) (139) (143) (144) (145)
Many times in our life when we are uncertain, we need to turn our hearts and even our words towards the goodness and sovereignty of God. By posturing our heart in humility towards the one true God, God's presence is drawn into our circumstances. What does God love and hate? What motivates God to do what He does?

Prayer
What is God saying to you? What do you need to say to God? Use a prayer model and your monthly prayer targets and requests as a guide.

DAY 147

Worship

Get alone with God. Find a quiet place. Sit down. Silence all distractions.

Scripture: 1 Chronicles ㉖ ㉗ ㉘ ㉙   Psalm ⟨127⟩

Consider the significance of the Temple and a permanent place for worship. Notice the details and those who are set apart for temple service. Imagine a time when something you loved that was temporary became permanent. God is establishing His people by providing a permanent place of worship foreshadowing a time when He will dwell in us as Christians.

Prayer

What is God saying to you? What do you need to say to God? Use a prayer model and your monthly prayer targets and requests as a guide.

COMMUNITY

I attended a church service this week (circle):   YES   NO

I shared my faith and talked about my church with others this week (circle):   YES   NO

I connected with other Christians in a smaller group this week. If yes, describe.

DAY 148

Worship
Get alone with God. Find a quiet place. Sit down. Silence all distractions.

Scripture: Psalm (111) (112) (113) (114) (115) (116) (117) (118)
The fear of the Lord is the beginning of all wisdom. The fear referenced is the idea of awe and respect. When we revere God and consider him in how we process life, we position ourselves to act in wisdom. What does it look like to practice the fear of the Lord each day? When we delight in who God is, we are happy because He changes our hearts.

Prayer
What is God saying to you? What do you need to say to God? Use a prayer model and your monthly prayer targets and requests as a guide.

DAY 149

Worship
Get alone with God. Find a quiet place. Sit down. Silence all distractions.

Scripture: 1 Kings (1) (2)   Psalm (37) (71) (94)
Even when others try to thwart the will of God, it never works. What God has established cannot be overturned, and that should give us great confidence since we know that God's will for us is good.

Prayer
What is God saying to you? What do you need to say to God? Use a prayer model and your monthly prayer targets and requests as a guide.

DAY 150

Worship
Get alone with God. Find a quiet place. Sit down. Silence all distractions.

Scripture: Psalm (119)
This chapter is the center of the Bible, and the longest chapter in all of scripture. Many people think that Ezra, the priest and scribe, wrote this Psalm. You can see how much the Psalmist loves God's word and understands God's Character. It is God who is the heart-changing agent of our lives. By leaning into God and His Word, our lives are transformed.

Prayer
What is God saying to you? What do you need to say to God? Use a prayer model and your monthly prayer targets and requests as a guide.

DAY 151

Worship
Get alone with God. Find a quiet place. Sit down. Silence all distractions.

Scripture: 1 Kings (3)(4)
Today, we see God's truth and pursuit of His creation. Even when we tend to forget, just like Solomon has, God is always showing us and reminding us that we belong to Him and everything we need is in Him. Though we sin and struggle to maintain a relationship with God at times, He desires for us to draw near to Him in everything we do.

Prayer
What is God saying to you? What do you need to say to God? Use a prayer model and your monthly prayer targets and requests as a guide.

DAY 152

Worship

Get alone with God. Find a quiet place. Sit down. Silence all distractions.

Scripture: 2 Chronicles (1)   Psalm (72)

God's generosity is more than riches and wealth; it's His heart toward each and every single one of us. Even when we fail to obey on our end, God always wants to show us His generosity through blessings to remind us of who He is. We see that He gives Solomon what He asks for and more. Ask God for the desires of your heart and ask Him to align them to His will for your life.

Prayer

What is God saying to you? What do you need to say to God? Use a prayer model and your monthly prayer targets and requests as a guide.

DAY 153

Worship

Get alone with God. Find a quiet place. Sit down. Silence all distractions.

Scripture: Song Of Solomon (1)(2)(3)(4)(5)(6)(7)(8)

God, our Creator, had good things in mind when He invented relationships, marriage, and sex. Like any inventor, He wants us to know how to use what He made so that we don't break or harm ourselves and others. When we use what God has given us for its intended purpose, it gives glory to God.

Prayer

What is God saying to you? What do you need to say to God? Use a prayer model and your monthly prayer targets and requests as a guide.

DAY 154

Worship
Get alone with God. Find a quiet place. Sit down. Silence all distractions.

Scripture: Proverbs ① ② ③
We know that God has always wanted to have a relationship with His creation. That it isn't a monologue but a dialogue, a conversation between God and His creation. He wants us to talk to Him about everything. Yes, He knows all, but it means so much more when He is included in the conversation. We see that He cares about us and wants us to live wisely through the experiences of Solomon.

Prayer
What is God saying to you? What do you need to say to God? Use a prayer model and your monthly prayer targets and requests as a guide.

COMMUNITY

I attended a church service this week (circle):   YES   NO

I shared my faith and talked about my church with others this week (circle):   YES   NO

I connected with other Christians in a smaller group this week.
If yes, describe.

DAY 155

Worship
Get alone with God. Find a quiet place. Sit down. Silence all distractions.

Scripture: Proverbs (4)(5)(6)
In today's reading, you'll notice there is a multitude of themes that are being presented to us, choices that we get to make on a regular basis. Our choices will either lead us down a road to destruction or to freedom and true life found in Jesus. Be mindful today as you make choices that affect your life.

Prayer
What is God saying to you? What do you need to say to God? Use a prayer model and your monthly prayer targets and requests as a guide.

DAY 156

Worship
Get alone with God. Find a quiet place. Sit down. Silence all distractions.

Scripture: Proverbs (7)(8)(9)
In today's reading, the father is encouraging the son to choose wisdom in compromising situations. Through this, we see God's mercy and grace. He provides a way out of every sinful circumstance, and because of this, we can choose the path of wisdom. Choose wisdom today in your conversations, interactions, and relationships.

Prayer
What is God saying to you? What do you need to say to God? Use a prayer model and your monthly prayer targets and requests as a guide.

DAY 157

Worship

Get alone with God. Find a quiet place. Sit down. Silence all distractions.

Scripture: Proverbs (10) (11) (12)

As you can see by now, this book is full of seeking truth and living wisely. Through this, we discover humility and righteousness, the right way. The humble person realizes that the wise thing to do is walk in God's ways, not their own. The righteous are not only blessed themselves, but also serve as a blessing to those around them. Today, take a moment and ask God to humble you and that you would live righteously for the benefit of blessing others.

Prayer

What is God saying to you? What do you need to say to God? Use a prayer model and your monthly prayer targets and requests as a guide.

DAY 158

Worship

Get alone with God. Find a quiet place. Sit down. Silence all distractions.

Scripture: Proverbs (13) (14) (15)

In today's reading, the father is encouraging the son to choose wisdom in suffering. Think about it, a wise person has often gained wisdom from their suffering. God doesn't want us to suffer in the same way that those who have gone before us have. In order for that to happen, we must apply what these proverbs are directing and teaching us to do. Ask God to draw you closer to Him today. Ask God for what you need, and He will reveal Himself to you.

Prayer

What is God saying to you? What do you need to say to God? Use a prayer model and your monthly prayer targets and requests as a guide.

DAY 159

Worship
Get alone with God. Find a quiet place. Sit down. Silence all distractions.

Scripture: Proverbs (16) (17) (18)
You never come into wisdom by accident. It's intentional. We see God is patient with us, even when we don't obey. He's a loving Father who waits for us, is ready and able to give us everything we need. He's working in everything to bring about the restoration of all the things we've broken. Ask God to search your heart today and reveal what needs to be restored in your life.

Prayer
What is God saying to you? What do you need to say to God? Use a prayer model and your monthly prayer targets and requests as a guide.

DAY 160

Worship
Get alone with God. Find a quiet place. Sit down. Silence all distractions.

Scripture: Proverbs (19) (20) (21)
In today's reading, we see God is relational and wants us to thrive in our relationships with others and with Him. Many people have a relationship with God that is only driven by emotion, unsupported by any knowledge of who He is, and tend to do the same with the relationships with the people around us. As you go on with your day, make it a point to be more intentional about how you're getting to know God and the people around you.

Prayer
What is God saying to you? What do you need to say to God? Use a prayer model and your monthly prayer targets and requests as a guide.

DAY 161

Worship
Get alone with God. Find a quiet place. Sit down. Silence all distractions.

Scripture: Proverbs (22) (23) (24)
You'll see God's mercy and grace in a huge way in today's reading. Usually when we experience "bad" people, we think that they get what they deserve when something "bad" happens to them, but God thinks differently. Remember, His thoughts and ways are higher. The same God who adopted you into His family is the same God who wants the best for those who seem the most undeserving. Let's be honest, none of us deserve what God gives, but He gives it to us freely and with love. Who is someone in your life who has treated you poorly that you can begin to pray for them?

Prayer
What is God saying to you? What do you need to say to God? Use a prayer model and your monthly prayer targets and requests as a guide.

COMMUNITY

I attended a church service this week (circle):   YES   NO

I shared my faith and talked about my church with others this week (circle):   YES   NO

I connected with other Christians in a smaller group this week.
If yes, describe.

DAY 162

Worship
Get alone with God. Find a quiet place. Sit down. Silence all distractions.

Scripture: 1 Kings (5)(6)   2 Chronicles (2)(3)
The reading today may seem like a list of architecture to-do's, but what we're seeing here is that God doesn't waste a thing. On the very same Mount is where in Genesis, we see Abraham offering Isaac before God stopped him and provided a sacrifice, and it also foreshadows the sacrifice of Jesus in the New Testament. God shows that the covenant relationship is based on hearts that demonstrate their love for Him through obedience. How can you show your love through obedience to God today?

Prayer
What is God saying to you? What do you need to say to God? Use a prayer model and your monthly prayer targets and requests as a guide.

DAY 163

Worship
Get alone with God. Find a quiet place. Sit down. Silence all distractions.

Scripture: 1 Kings (7)   2 Chronicles (4)
God doesn't break His promises. What he sets out to do, He will finish. Even when all of the things we've built, jobs, a decorated home, a financially secured life, etc. It can all come to an end but what we see is that God still remains. His presence will always be with us if we allow it. God doesn't dwell in our belongings and assets; He dwells in us.

Prayer
What is God saying to you? What do you need to say to God? Use a prayer model and your monthly prayer targets and requests as a guide.

DAY 164

Worship
Get alone with God. Find a quiet place. Sit down. Silence all distractions.

Scripture: 1 Kings (8)   2 Chronicles (5)
Sometimes we can miss the mark or embellish something God spoke to us, but even in that, we see God has a sense of humor. Just as Solomon completed the Temple, he said, "...a place for you to dwell forever." God never said that even though the sentiment was thoughtful. God wants to live in us so we can live whole.

Prayer
What is God saying to you? What do you need to say to God? Use a prayer model and your monthly prayer targets and requests as a guide.

DAY 165

Worship
Get alone with God. Find a quiet place. Sit down. Silence all distractions.

Scripture: 2 Chronicles (6) (7)   Psalm (136)
It's easy to fixate on specific consequences from God and wonder why a loving God would do that. Keep in mind that consequences only happen when there is disobedience. Cherry-picking the Bible can be dangerous, remember that God chooses to love us even when we don't deserve it. It is remarkable that God comes down to live with us, dwell in us, and concentrate His perfect love on us even in the midst of our disobedience. Ask God to show you the truth in its fullness and not what's convenient for you.

Prayer
What is God saying to you? What do you need to say to God? Use a prayer model and your monthly prayer targets and requests as a guide.

DAY 166

Get alone with God. Find a quiet place. Sit down. Silence all distractions.

Scripture: Psalm (134) (146) (147) (148) (149) (150)
Today's reading is a great reminder of where our identity and fulfillment in life comes from. We cannot place our value in people or expect them to fulfill us the way that only God can. Not that this a directive to be suspicious or cynical to everyone meet moving forward, but as a reminder that we are to look to God for what we need and who we are. It's easy to get lost amongst the crowd, but God sees you exactly where you are.

Prayer
What is God saying to you? What do you need to say to God? Use a prayer model and your monthly prayer targets and requests as a guide.

DAY 167

Worship
Get alone with God. Find a quiet place. Sit down. Silence all distractions.

Scripture: 1 Kings (9)   2 Chronicles (8)
Have you ever wondered where you stood with someone and your relationship with them? Thankfully, we don't have to worry when it comes to God. He tells us that we're loved, and we must also obey Him. It's a gracious gift that He gives to us every day. Sometimes you need to be reminded that you are loved by God and that you don't need to strive to make Him love you more. Discover that today as you read.

Prayer
What is God saying to you? What do you need to say to God? Use a prayer model and your monthly prayer targets and requests as a guide.

DAY 168

Worship
Get alone with God. Find a quiet place. Sit down. Silence all distractions.

Scripture: Proverbs (25) (26)
Timing seems to be a big problem for many of us. Patience is a fruit of The Spirit that many of us are still learning to grow. Whether if it's waiting for something to happen or to know a certain bit of information, we tend to rush the process. God is intentional with His timing and details. He reveals at the perfect time, but we must ask Him to develop patience. So, go ahead, and ask Him today!

Prayer
What is God saying to you? What do you need to say to God? Use a prayer model and your monthly prayer targets and requests as a guide.

COMMUNITY

I attended a church service this week (circle):   YES   NO

I shared my faith and talked about my church with others this week (circle):   YES   NO

I connected with other Christians in a smaller group this week.
If yes, describe.

DAY 169

Worship
Get alone with God. Find a quiet place. Sit down. Silence all distractions.

Scripture: Proverbs (27) (28) (29)
Our mind-set determines much of what we will do throughout a day. If you feel exhausted, you'll generally choose the activities that use the least amount of energy. In today's reading, we're challenged with the mind-set of the righteous versus the wicked. Ask God to remind you that His Spirit is within you and equips you for everything He allows into your life.

Prayer
What is God saying to you? What do you need to say to God? Use a prayer model and your monthly prayer targets and requests as a guide.

DAY 170

Worship
Get alone with God. Find a quiet place. Sit down. Silence all distractions.

Scripture: Ecclesiastes (1) (2) (3) (4) (5) (6)
In today's reading, we are reminded that the things we strive to gain are fleeting and we exhaust ourselves. Everything that God sets and makes happen will last. It's eternal and won't be shaken. That has to bring relief to mind and take weight off your shoulders. Simply ask God to remind you that He is in control and that it is better that way.

Prayer
What is God saying to you? What do you need to say to God? Use a prayer model and your monthly prayer targets and requests as a guide.

DAY 171

Worship
Get alone with God. Find a quiet place. Sit down. Silence all distractions.

Scripture: Ecclesiastes ⑦ ⑧ ⑨ ⑩ ⑪ ⑫
Death is never a fun topic to discuss or think about, but when we look at it from a fresh perspective, it can be encouraging. We cannot control the outcome of death, but we can choose how to live with the days we are given and trust God with the outcome. We think that having the best cars, homes, wardrobe, etc. will give us the best life there is, but as the author says in today's reading, no amount of anything on earth can compare or touch the peace and joy that comes from humbly walking with God.

Prayer
What is God saying to you? What do you need to say to God? Use a prayer model and your monthly prayer targets and requests as a guide.

DAY 172

Worship
Get alone with God. Find a quiet place. Sit down. Silence all distractions.

Scripture: 1 Kings ⑩ ⑪   2 Chronicles ⑨
In today's reading, take time to reflect on what you can discover about God's character and what God is doing in these scriptures. Remember, everything in His word points back to Him and who He is.

Prayer
What is God saying to you? What do you need to say to God? Use a prayer model and your monthly prayer targets and requests as a guide.

DAY 173

Worship
Get alone with God. Find a quiet place. Sit down. Silence all distractions.

Scripture: Proverbs (30) (31)
Your life should reflect who you desire to be like. The purpose of Proverbs 31 isn't to place a standard that is unreachable for women or for comparison. It encourages women to find their strength, belonging, identity, and purpose in God. When she does, her life radiates God and others recognize it. What is one thing you can focus on with God today that would reflect Him to others?

Prayer
What is God saying to you? What do you need to say to God? Use a prayer model and your monthly prayer targets and requests as a guide.

DAY 174

Worship
Get alone with God. Find a quiet place. Sit down. Silence all distractions.

Scripture: 1 Kings (12) (13) (14)
Today's reading maybe a bit confusing with a lot of information but stay with us. Seek and find God in the scriptures you're reading. Find the moral and lesson God wants you to learn today. God's voice brings unity and understanding. Be mindful when you allow people to speak into your life, and make sure you go to God for the truth.

Prayer
What is God saying to you? What do you need to say to God? Use a prayer model and your monthly prayer targets and requests as a guide.

DAY 175

Worship

Get alone with God. Find a quiet place. Sit down. Silence all distractions.

Scripture: 2 Chronicles (10) (11) (12)

Here's a thought for you before you start reading. Isn't it amazing that with God, when you surrender, you actually gain? God takes things from us, gives us difficult assignments, places tough relationships in our lives, not because He's upset with us. He wants to give us an opportunity to surrender to Him, and He always comes through. Think about how you can surrender to God today.

Prayer

What is God saying to you? What do you need to say to God? Use a prayer model and your monthly prayer targets and requests as a guide.

COMMUNITY

I attended a church service this week (circle):   YES   NO

I shared my faith and talked about my church with others this week (circle):   YES   NO

I connected with other Christians in a smaller group this week.
If yes, describe.

DAY 176

Worship
Get alone with God. Find a quiet place. Sit down. Silence all distractions.

Scripture: 1 Kings (15)   2 Chronicles (13) (14) (15) (16)
Take time to write down what you see God doing in today's reading. Where do you see God in these scriptures? What does it say about who God is? What does God say about you?

Prayer
What is God saying to you? What do you need to say to God? Use a prayer model and your monthly prayer targets and requests as a guide.

DAY 177

Worship
Get alone with God. Find a quiet place. Sit down. Silence all distractions.

Scripture: 1 Kings (16)   2 Chronicles (17)
Think about this while you read; even though we cannot see it, it doesn't mean that God isn't doing something behind the scenes. You'll see God's sovereignty because He does a lot of work on a heart level, from the inside out. Something in us must change before the things around us change. What needs to change in your heart before circumstances can change around you?

Prayer
What is God saying to you? What do you need to say to God? Use a prayer model and your monthly prayer targets and requests as a guide.

DAY 178

Worship

Get alone with God. Find a quiet place. Sit down. Silence all distractions.

Scripture: 1 Kings (17) (18) (19)

Most people imagine God is so big that He can never relate to individuals on a personal level, but that's not true. You'll see in today's reading that God can use massive displays of power but wants to show us that He is relational, unlike the pagan gods. He's in the thunder, but He's also in the whisper. Wanting to be intimate with us. He's a loving and relational God. Take a moment and be still today. Allow God to speak to you.

Prayer

What is God saying to you? What do you need to say to God? Use a prayer model and your monthly prayer targets and requests as a guide.

DAY 179

Worship

Get alone with God. Find a quiet place. Sit down. Silence all distractions.

Scripture: 1 Kings (20) (21)

God is faithful and keeps His promises. When you read, you'll notice Ahab fails and disobeys, but God relaxes His punishment because he displayed repentance. This is a great example of how eager and willing God is to forgive, but we must first choose to turn our hearts from sin. Reflect on how God has done this for you when you didn't deserve it.

Prayer

What is God saying to you? What do you need to say to God? Use a prayer model and your monthly prayer targets and requests as a guide.

DAY 180

Worship

Get alone with God. Find a quiet place. Sit down. Silence all distractions.

Scripture: 1 King (22)   2 Chronicles (18)

Think about this today as you read; as humans, we have a tendency to change our mind, but God's plan is set in stone. It's easy to feel like control is lost when someone in power or authority moves in a different direction than planned. Thankfully, we serve a God who can't be thwarted, no matter the circumstances.

Prayer

What is God saying to you? What do you need to say to God? Use a prayer model and your monthly prayer targets and requests as a guide.

DAY 181

Worship

Get alone with God. Find a quiet place. Sit down. Silence all distractions.

Scripture: 2 Chronicles (19) (20) (21) (22) (23)

Never underestimate the power of prayer and talking with God. Remember what we saw yesterday, God is not shaken by our circumstances. No matter what terrible things happen, remember that you're in a relationship with a trustworthy God. Go to God in prayer today and thank Him in advance for what you're facing today!

Prayer

What is God saying to you? What do you need to say to God? Use a prayer model and your monthly prayer targets and requests as a guide.

DAY 182

Worship

Get alone with God. Find a quiet place. Sit down. Silence all distractions.

Scripture: Obadiah (1)   Psalm (82) (83)

You're halfway through! That's amazing, and we encourage you to keep going! Today, you'll see that God is very personal and protective. God identifies so closely with His people that when they're mistreated, He takes it personally. The thing is, God doesn't seek revenge but instead, His vengeance is perfect and just. His ways and thoughts are higher.

Prayer

What is God saying to you? What do you need to say to God? Use a prayer model and your monthly prayer targets and requests as a guide.

COMMUNITY

I attended a church service this week (circle):   YES   NO

I shared my faith and talked about my church with others this week (circle):   YES   NO

I connected with other Christians in a smaller group this week. If yes, describe.

DAY 183

Worship
Get alone with God. Find a quiet place. Sit down. Silence all distractions.

Scripture: 2 Kings (1) (2) (3) (4)
Take time to think about the last 182 days of reading. What have you learned about God? What have you learned about yourself? What are you excited about for this second half?

Prayer
What is God saying to you? What do you need to say to God? Use a prayer model and your monthly prayer targets and requests as a guide.

DAY 184

Worship
Get alone with God. Find a quiet place. Sit down. Silence all distractions.

Scripture: 2 Kings (5) (6) (7) (8)
Here's something to think about today. Sometimes God does things that baffles the mind and logic. Who pursues their enemy to bless them? God does. He sets out to seek an enemy who doubts Him to show them how real He is. It's the heart of God, His kindness, that leads us to repentance. Showing kindness costs nothing, and it benefits so many. Ask God for His eyes and heart today as you interact with others at work, the grocery store, coffee shop, and at home.

Prayer
What is God saying to you? What do you need to say to God? Use a prayer model and your monthly prayer targets and requests as a guide.

DAY 185

Worship
Get alone with God. Find a quiet place. Sit down. Silence all distractions.

Scripture: 2 Kings ⑨ ⑩ ⑪
There are times it feels like God isn't present. We feel alone or abandoned, but that's far from the truth. God is at work in the background, doing things the eyes cannot see or fathom. He is providing for the future ahead and preparing our hearts today.

Prayer
What is God saying to you? What do you need to say to God? Use a prayer model and your monthly prayer targets and requests as a guide.

DAY 186

Worship
Get alone with God. Find a quiet place. Sit down. Silence all distractions.

Scripture: 2 Kings ⑫ ⑬   2 Chronicles ㉔
God is exclusive and inclusive. You see, God doesn't need our help, but He wants us to help. Yes, He can accomplish every plan He has without the help of humans, but He's much more loving than that. His power and goodness aren't contingent on our strengths or our faith, but He does include us.

Prayer
What is God saying to you? What do you need to say to God? Use a prayer model and your monthly prayer targets and requests as a guide.

DAY 187

Worship

Get alone with God. Find a quiet place. Sit down. Silence all distractions.

Scripture: 2 Kings ⑭   2 Chronicles ㉕

You'll see in today's reading that God is victorious. He isn't passive about His will and what He sets out to do in Heaven and Earth. Time and time again, no one will get in the way, and the victory belongs to The Lord. Where in your life have you seen God be victorious? How do you identify God's victories?

Prayer

What is God saying to you? What do you need to say to God? Use a prayer model and your monthly prayer targets and requests as a guide.

DAY 188

Worship

Get alone with God. Find a quiet place. Sit down. Silence all distractions.

Scripture: Jonah ① ② ③ ④

All of us can relate to Jonah's life. God gives direction, we don't like it, and run in the opposite direction. We may even pick out the parts we like the best and run with that. Partial obedience is still disobedience; there isn't a gray area with this. Thankfully, we have God's steadfast and patient love for us. Is there something in your life you haven't been obedient with?

Prayer

What is God saying to you? What do you need to say to God? Use a prayer model and your monthly prayer targets and requests as a guide.

DAY 189

Worship
Get alone with God. Find a quiet place. Sit down. Silence all distractions.

Scripture: 2 Kings ⑮   2 Chronicles ㉖
So many of God's attributes are on display in today's reading. You'll see that no one will get in the way of God's plan and will, but He will also show His mercy. What a great reminder of who our God is. Take that into your day!

Prayer
What is God saying to you? What do you need to say to God? Use a prayer model and your monthly prayer targets and requests as a guide.

COMMUNITY

I attended a church service this week (circle):   YES   NO

I shared my faith and talked about my church with others this week (circle):   YES   NO

I connected with other Christians in a smaller group this week.
If yes, describe.

DAY 190

Worship

Get alone with God. Find a quiet place. Sit down. Silence all distractions.

Scripture: Isaiah ① ② ③ ④

Today, we're given the imagery of the many ways God is present with His people, even if they aren't with Him. Sometimes when God feels so distant, He's closer than you know. What are you noticing about God's proximity throughout these chapters?

Prayer

What is God saying to you? What do you need to say to God? Use a prayer model and your monthly prayer targets and requests as a guide.

DAY 191

Worship

Get alone with God. Find a quiet place. Sit down. Silence all distractions.

Scripture: Isaiah ⑤ ⑥ ⑦ ⑧

Look for Jesus in today's reading because there's more foreshadowing of Jesus in these scriptures. God's throne is in the Temple, not in a palace. Kingship and priesthood merge, and that directs us to Jesus. This shows us that God has always had a plan for humanity's redemption.

Prayer

What is God saying to you? What do you need to say to God? Use a prayer model and your monthly prayer targets and requests as a guide.

DAY 192

Worship
Get alone with God. Find a quiet place. Sit down. Silence all distractions.

Scripture: Amos (1) (2) (3) (4) (5)
This is a lot to take in today, so take your time reading. We feel like the enemy may have the upper hand, but God is just, and He wouldn't be God if He ignored sin and evil. He is faithful, even when we're not. He is patient, even when we're not. He is trustworthy, even when we're not.

Prayer
What is God saying to you? What do you need to say to God? Use a prayer model and your monthly prayer targets and requests as a guide.

DAY 193

Worship
Get alone with God. Find a quiet place. Sit down. Silence all distractions.

Scripture: Amos (6) (7) (8) (9)
We will be reading heavy stuff today, but in a great way because God's goal with punishment is always restoration. In the moment, the punishment doesn't feel good, but it is necessary to move forward to restore what wasn't done the first time. Everything God is about to put Israel through, He went through Himself. It seems unfair, right? The most unfair part of this is that we never have to receive the punishment for sin, because Jesus paid that price for us. What does this tell you about God?

Prayer
What is God saying to you? What do you need to say to God? Use a prayer model and your monthly prayer targets and requests as a guide.

DAY 194

Worship
Get alone with God. Find a quiet place. Sit down. Silence all distractions.

Scripture: 2 Chronicles ㉗   Isaiah ⑨ ⑩ ⑪ ⑫
Try this and place yourself in their shoes, or sandals, for a moment. After facing so much war and oppression, you'd find it hard to believe that peace was on its way. The punishment they were facing because of their sin was brutal, but it was needed in order to restore what God promised. The peace of Jesus was promised, but their present was punishment. Is there an area of your life you need to surrender to God so your life can be restored?

Prayer
What is God saying to you? What do you need to say to God? Use a prayer model and your monthly prayer targets and requests as a guide.

DAY 195

Worship
Get alone with God. Find a quiet place. Sit down. Silence all distractions.

Scripture: Micah ① ② ③ ④ ⑤ ⑥ ⑦
Look for a constant reminder throughout Micah that God will preserve a remnant, and the Savior will come from among them. Even in the middle of destruction, God shows great mercy in efforts to have them turn their hearts back to Him. God wants to include us, but we sometimes have to face the hard stuff in life because of our own choices. Spend time with God today and ask Him to reveal truth in your life more than ever.

Prayer
What is God saying to you? What do you need to say to God? Use a prayer model and your monthly prayer targets and requests as a guide.

DAY 196

Worship
Get alone with God. Find a quiet place. Sit down. Silence all distractions.

Scripture: 2 Chronicles (28)   2 Kings (16) (17)
You'll see in today's reading that the warnings given to Israel and Judah were over centuries. It wasn't in one day; it was hundreds of years of being warned of what would happen if they continued to live in disobedience. That definitely shows God's patience. He still remains the same today. Is there something God has warned you about and you continue to do? What do you need to do in order to live in obedience?

Prayer
What is God saying to you? What do you need to say to God? Use a prayer model and your monthly prayer targets and requests as a guide.

COMMUNITY

I attended a church service this week (circle):   YES   NO

I shared my faith and talked about my church with others this week (circle):   YES   NO

I connected with other Christians in a smaller group this week.
If yes, describe.

DAY 197

Worship

Get alone with God. Find a quiet place. Sit down. Silence all distractions.

Scripture: Isaiah (13) (14) (15) (16) (17)

Ask yourself these questions today while you read. What did you discover about God? What does this say about God? How does this apply to your life?

Prayer

What is God saying to you? What do you need to say to God? Use a prayer model and your monthly prayer targets and requests as a guide.

DAY 198

Worship

Get alone with God. Find a quiet place. Sit down. Silence all distractions.

Scripture: Isaiah (18) (19) (20) (21) (22)

We continue to see nations being warned about the punishment that will come their way if they do not repent. God shows Himself as sovereign, not just over nations or the world, but over thoughts and words. Sounds interesting, but if you think about it, that's what the Holy Spirit is for. To guide our hearts, thoughts, words in the truth. Ask the Holy Spirit to guide your conversations and interactions today.

Prayer

What is God saying to you? What do you need to say to God? Use a prayer model and your monthly prayer targets and requests as a guide.

DAY 199

Worship
Get alone with God. Find a quiet place. Sit down. Silence all distractions.

Scripture: Isaiah ㉓ ㉔ ㉕ ㉖ ㉗
Take this with you while you read today. Judgment, it doesn't sound like a nice word. It sounds harsh, but the truth is that it's real. Whether we like it or not, judgment is happening. No one knows when, but it will come. That tells us that God is purposeful. He wouldn't create billions of people on the earth without having a purpose for every individual. How amazing is that? God cares about every single detail of every single human He created. He created us so He will sustain us. All we need to do is trust and follow Him.

Prayer
What is God saying to you? What do you need to say to God? Use a prayer model and your monthly prayer targets and requests as a guide.

DAY 200

Worship
Get alone with God. Find a quiet place. Sit down. Silence all distractions.

Scripture: 2 Kings ⑱   2 Chronicles ㉙ ㉚ ㉛   Psalm ㊽
You'll see in today's reading God is after our hearts, not the rituals. We can check off every box we think we need to in order to satisfy God, but that means nothing if our hearts aren't in it. The rituals and practices become shallow actions because God looks at the heart. Ask God to show you your heart. To really dig deep and show you what He sees.

Prayer
What is God saying to you? What do you need to say to God? Use a prayer model and your monthly prayer targets and requests as a guide.

DAY 201

Worship
Get alone with God. Find a quiet place. Sit down. Silence all distractions.

Scripture: Hosea (1) (2) (3) (4) (5) (6) (7)
In Hosea, we read that Israel has forgotten all about God and committed idolatry once again. The truth is, sin exists in all of us, and it must be punished. However, when we truly worship God, accept Christ as our Savior, and make him the Lord of our lives, God forgives our sin and welcomes us into his family.

Prayer
What is God saying to you? What do you need to say to God? Use a prayer model and your monthly prayer targets and requests as a guide.

DAY 202

Worship
Get alone with God. Find a quiet place. Sit down. Silence all distractions.

Scripture: Hosea (8) (9) (10) (11) (12) (13) (14)
In today's reading, we get a glimpse of God's heart for his children. In Chapter 11, God is infuriated with Israel and their never-ending track record of idolatry. We will see God's attitude towards Israel shift in verse 8: "My heart is torn within me and my compassion overflows." In spite of our sin, God's heart towards us will always be full of compassion and mercy.

Prayer
What is God saying to you? What do you need to say to God? Use a prayer model and your monthly prayer targets and requests as a guide.

DAY 203

Worship
Get alone with God. Find a quiet place. Sit down. Silence all distractions.

Scripture: Isaiah ㉘ ㉙ ㉚
As you read today, take a look at how God describes himself in Chapter 30:20-21: You will see your teacher with your own eyes. Your own ears will hear him. We see here that God's heart isn't to rebuke us and leave us to figure it out for ourselves. No, God wants to lead us, teach us, and guide us closer to him.

Prayer
What is God saying to you? What do you need to say to God? Use a prayer model and your monthly prayer targets and requests as a guide.

COMMUNITY

I attended a church service this week (circle):   YES   NO

I shared my faith and talked about my church with others this week (circle):   YES   NO

I connected with other Christians in a smaller group this week.
If yes, describe.

DAY 204

Worship

Get alone with God. Find a quiet place. Sit down. Silence all distractions.

Scripture: Isaiah (31) (32) (33) (34)

In today's reading, God shows us how his righteousness can transform our circumstances. Righteousness only comes from God, and "this righteousness will bring peace. Yes, it will bring quietness and confidence forever." This righteousness we read about brings peace and comfort to our situation!

Prayer

What is God saying to you? What do you need to say to God? Use a prayer model and your monthly prayer targets and requests as a guide.

DAY 205

Worship

Get alone with God. Find a quiet place. Sit down. Silence all distractions.

Scripture: Isaiah (35) (36)

As you read today, take a look at how God is revealing his character through the prophecies of Isaiah. Isaiah writes about God's fulfillment, which means: the achievement of something desired, promised, or "predicted." Like the desert that blooms with an abundance of flowers, God makes the impossible possible and keeps every one of his promises.

Prayer

What is God saying to you? What do you need to say to God? Use a prayer model and your monthly prayer targets and requests as a guide.

DAY 206

Worship
Get alone with God. Find a quiet place. Sit down. Silence all distractions.

Scripture: Isaiah (37) (38) (39)   Psalm (76)
In today's reading, you'll see God's sovereignty in action through the story of King Sennacherib. Though he was a powerful king and enemy of God, he didn't stand a chance against God's plan for Israel and the victories that would take place. God's plans for our lives are meant to bless us and comfort, because he sees us as his children!

Prayer
What is God saying to you? What do you need to say to God? Use a prayer model and your monthly prayer targets and requests as a guide.

DAY 207

Worship
Get alone with God. Find a quiet place. Sit down. Silence all distractions.

Scripture: Isaiah (40) (41) (42) (43)
As you read today, notice how God refers to Israel, Jacob, and Abraham. He calls Israel "my servant," Jacob "chosen, and Abraham "friend." Each of these had faults: Israel rebelled and sinned repeatedly, Jacob used trickery to steal Esau's blessing, and Abraham struggled with surrendering to God's timing. Regardless of our sins and mistakes, God welcomes us into his family as we are.

Prayer
What is God saying to you? What do you need to say to God? Use a prayer model and your monthly prayer targets and requests as a guide.

DAY 208

Worship
Get alone with God. Find a quiet place. Sit down. Silence all distractions.

Scripture: Isaiah (44) (45) (46) (47) (48)
God clarifies his heart towards us in Isaiah 45:19. He says, "I do not whisper obscurities in some dark corner. I would not have told the people of Israel to seek me if I could not be found." Not one prayer, not one second of attention we give God, is useless. Our desire to have a relationship with God delights him, and he gladly meets us where we are.

Prayer
What is God saying to you? What do you need to say to God? Use a prayer model and your monthly prayer targets and requests as a guide.

DAY 209

Worship
Get alone with God. Find a quiet place. Sit down. Silence all distractions.

Scripture: 2 Kings (19)   Psalm (46) (80) (135)
In today's reading, we read that God truly has a desire to bless His people. In Psalm 135, we read about the countless good things God has done to pour out his love on us. And, he does it willingly. It pleases God to adopt us into His family and show compassion towards us.

Prayer
What is God saying to you? What do you need to say to God? Use a prayer model and your monthly prayer targets and requests as a guide.

DAY 210

Worship
Get alone with God. Find a quiet place. Sit down. Silence all distractions.

Scripture: Isaiah (49) (50) (51) (52) (53)
In today's reading, it can become easy to place our emotions and feelings on how God should feel. Jesus is being spoken about even before He appears on the scene. His future and fate was already sealed because of God's plan to redeem humanity.

Prayer
What is God saying to you? What do you need to say to God? Use a prayer model and your monthly prayer targets and requests as a guide.

COMMUNITY

I attended a church service this week (circle):   YES   NO

I shared my faith and talked about my church with others this week
(circle):   YES   NO

I connected with other Christians in a smaller group this week.
If yes, describe.

DAY 211

Worship
Get alone with God. Find a quiet place. Sit down. Silence all distractions.

Scripture: Isaiah (54) (55) (56) (57) (58)
In today's reading, you'll read a small passage that lays out God's heart towards those who choose to repent towards Him. 57:15 says, "I restore the crushed spirit of the humble and revive the courage of those with repentant hearts." As you read this passage, reflect on your own life and remember that God wants to be near to you and bring you peace.

Prayer
What is God saying to you? What do you need to say to God? Use a prayer model and your monthly prayer targets and requests as a guide.

DAY 212

Worship
Get alone with God. Find a quiet place. Sit down. Silence all distractions.

Scripture: Isaiah (59) (60) (61) (62) (63)
As you read today, notice how chapter 61 sets up the role of Jesus Christ in our lives. We see prophetic proof of God's heart for us in verse 1: Jesus came to free us, release us, and comfort us. These truths are scattered all throughout these prophecies to build our faith and remind us of God's compassion for us, as his children.

Prayer
What is God saying to you? What do you need to say to God? Use a prayer model and your monthly prayer targets and requests as a guide.

DAY 213

Worship

Get alone with God. Find a quiet place. Sit down. Silence all distractions.

Scripture: Isaiah (64) (65) (66)

In today's reading, we get a further explanation of God's plan for salvation and judgment. What you'll notice is that God is outspoken about his thoughts on the "new heavens" and "new earth" he's determined to create. God isn't looking to send another flood or burn cities to the ground. Instead, God's heart is to restore all of creation. He does this in us, too: He restores us and makes us new when we surrender to him.

Prayer

What is God saying to you? What do you need to say to God? Use a prayer model and your monthly prayer targets and requests as a guide.

DAY 214

Worship

Get alone with God. Find a quiet place. Sit down. Silence all distractions.

Scripture: 2 Kings (20) (21)

As you read today, don't read too quickly over Hezekiah's prayer to God in 20:3. You may read to yourself and think: "Was God's original message to Hezekiah a lie." Of course not! This is actually an example of how our prayers function in our relationship with the Father. Prayer isn't just about getting what we want from God. They're about getting close to God.

Prayer

What is God saying to you? What do you need to say to God? Use a prayer model and your monthly prayer targets and requests as a guide.

DAY 215

Worship

Get alone with God. Find a quiet place. Sit down. Silence all distractions.

Scripture: 2 Chronicles ㉜ ㉝

As you read today, pay attention to Hezekiah's encouragement to the people of Judah. This encouragement and reminder are perhaps exactly what his military officials needed to carry on. His encouragement was to be "strong and courageous" and remember that God was on their side. This holds true no matter what we're facing. God is in the midst of our battles and never fails to leave our side.

Prayer

What is God saying to you? What do you need to say to God? Use a prayer model and your monthly prayer targets and requests as a guide.

DAY 216

Worship

Get alone with God. Find a quiet place. Sit down. Silence all distractions.

Scripture: Nahum ① ② ③

In today's reading, you may notice that the bulk of the reading is negative and targeted towards Nineveh. But in the middle of chapter 1, we see the contrast in God's protection over his people and his determination to destroy His enemies. His power has no end, and he will always fight for those who love him. In fact, when we can put our trust in Him, he draws near to us.

Prayer

What is God saying to you? What do you need to say to God? Use a prayer model and your monthly prayer targets and requests as a guide.

DAY 217

Worship
Get alone with God. Find a quiet place. Sit down. Silence all distractions.

Scripture: 2 Kings ㉒ ㉓   2 Chronicles ㉞ ㉟
In today's reading, we read about Josiah's realization when reading through the Word of the Law. In this moment, the weight of generation after generation of sin and disobedience hits him. This reality-check gives Josiah the revelation he needs to lead the people of Judah back towards God. No length of time and no distance is too far away that God can't continue to work in our lives and draw near to us.

Prayer
What is God saying to you? What do you need to say to God? Use a prayer model and your monthly prayer targets and requests as a guide.

COMMUNITY

I attended a church service this week (circle):   YES   NO

I shared my faith and talked about my church with others this week (circle):   YES   NO

I connected with other Christians in a smaller group this week.
If yes, describe.

DAY 218

Worship

Get alone with God. Find a quiet place. Sit down. Silence all distractions.

Scripture: Zephaniah (1) (2) (3)

For today's reading, take a look at how Zephaniah articulates repentance. He makes it simple to understand: Seek the Lord, follow his commands, do the right thing, and have a humble heart. Even though the nation of Judah remains to be proud, arrogant, and unrighteous, God's patience never runs out. And even when we find ourselves in the wrong place or believing the lies of the enemy, God never fails to be patient with us.

Prayer

What is God saying to you? What do you need to say to God? Use a prayer model and your monthly prayer targets and requests as a guide.

DAY 219

Worship

Get alone with God. Find a quiet place. Sit down. Silence all distractions.

Scripture: Jeremiah (1) (2) (3)

In today's reading, we read about Jeremiah and God's plan to use him. 1:10 reads: "Today I appoint you to stand up against nations and kingdoms. Some you must uproot and tear down, destroy and overthrow. Others you must build up and plant." God doesn't just want to destroy every nation and settle with the victory. Instead, God sees the value in taking broken things (even us, sometimes) and restoring them into greatness.

Prayer

What is God saying to you? What do you need to say to God? Use a prayer model and your monthly prayer targets and requests as a guide.

DAY 220

Worship
Get alone with God. Find a quiet place. Sit down. Silence all distractions.

Scripture: Jeremiah ④ ⑤ ⑥
Have you ever heard the phrase, "the way to a man's heart is through his stomach?" Well, in today's reading we get a small hint of how to make it to God's heart. In chapter 4, the Lord tells Jeremiah that "my people are foolish and do not know me." God doesn't just want us to follow his commands and do what He says. He wants an intimate relationship with each of us: one that openly welcomes His presence in our lives.

Prayer
What is God saying to you? What do you need to say to God? Use a prayer model and your monthly prayer targets and requests as a guide.

DAY 221

Worship
Get alone with God. Find a quiet place. Sit down. Silence all distractions.

Scripture: Jeremiah ⑦ ⑧ ⑨
In today's reading, God speaks out against the sins of the people of Judah. At this point in time, they are breaking almost all of the original commandments: stealing, lying, cheating, hurting one another, and idolizing things other than God. The holy Temple still stands, but God condemns them anyway. It was never about the Temple, or even doing the right thing. What God really wanted above all else is for their hearts to be fully devoted to him.

Prayer
What is God saying to you? What do you need to say to God? Use a prayer model and your monthly prayer targets and requests as a guide.

DAY 222

Worship
Get alone with God. Find a quiet place. Sit down. Silence all distractions.

Scripture: Jeremiah ⑩ ⑪ ⑫ ⑬
As you read today, notice how the people of Judah are still continuing down a dark and wicked path. And meanwhile, God still waits patiently for them to turn back towards them, knowing that they won't and that their sin will deserve punishment. This is a reminder that even when we are struggling and facing difficulties, God is in every moment, patiently waiting for us to turn from our own ways and turn towards him.

Prayer
What is God saying to you? What do you need to say to God? Use a prayer model and your monthly prayer targets and requests as a guide.

DAY 223

Worship
Get alone with God. Find a quiet place. Sit down. Silence all distractions.

Scripture: Jeremiah ⑭ ⑮ ⑯ ⑰
At this point in our reading, God begins to reveal that he is "fed up" with the people of Judah. God encourages Jeremiah to stay true to his purpose: to lead the people closer to God. Regardless of what our circumstances are, God calls us to not be influenced by the world, but to live in it and influence others for His glory.

Prayer
What is God saying to you? What do you need to say to God? Use a prayer model and your monthly prayer targets and requests as a guide.

DAY 224

Worship
Get alone with God. Find a quiet place. Sit down. Silence all distractions.

Scripture: Jeremiah (18) (19) (20) (21) (22)
In today's reading, we get another reminder that what wins God over is a heart fully devoted to him. The natural lineage of Israel was important, but that did not dictate God's heart towards them. Instead, God clarifies that His family is not strictly Israelites, but people who know God and trust him with their lives.

Prayer
What is God saying to you? What do you need to say to God? Use a prayer model and your monthly prayer targets and requests as a guide.

COMMUNITY

I attended a church service this week (circle):   YES   NO

I shared my faith and talked about my church with others this week (circle):   YES   NO

I connected with other Christians in a smaller group this week.
If yes, describe.

DAY 225

Worship
Get alone with God. Find a quiet place. Sit down. Silence all distractions.

Scripture: Jeremiah (23) (24) (25)
As you read today, take a minute to reflect on the past several days of reading. Notice how God makes it abundantly clear that he's after our hearts and our devotion, not just our actions. As you continue, remember that these readings aren't just meant to give you more knowledge of the Bible, but to strengthen your relationship with God through the process.

Prayer
What is God saying to you? What do you need to say to God? Use a prayer model and your monthly prayer targets and requests as a guide.

DAY 226

Worship
Get alone with God. Find a quiet place. Sit down. Silence all distractions.

Scripture: Jeremiah (26) (27) (28) (29)
In today's reading, God speaks again through Jeremiah to the people, priests, and kings, of Judah. The pattern we've seen through the past several days is that God's words are worth listening to. Whenever God speaks to us through His Word, we should never take that for granted.

Prayer
What is God saying to you? What do you need to say to God? Use a prayer model and your monthly prayer targets and requests as a guide.

DAY 227

Worship
Get alone with God. Find a quiet place. Sit down. Silence all distractions.

Scripture: Jeremiah ③⓪ ③①
In today's reading, look at how God describes His relationship with His people. He says, "Even though my people betray me and I punish them, I still love them. I will have mercy on them." In the depths of our sin, God never fails to give us mercy and love that we feel we don't deserve. That's because he is a good Father!

Prayer
What is God saying to you? What do you need to say to God? Use a prayer model and your monthly prayer targets and requests as a guide.

DAY 228

Worship
Get alone with God. Find a quiet place. Sit down. Silence all distractions.

Scripture: Jeremiah ③② ③③ ③④
As you read today, focus on the ideas presented in chapter 32. God says, "And I will give them one heart and one purpose: to worship me forever, for their own good and for the good of all their descendants." This is a beautiful picture of what the Local Church is supposed to look like. Though we're made up of different parts, we all share a common goal: to glorify God and help others know him.

Prayer
What is God saying to you? What do you need to say to God? Use a prayer model and your monthly prayer targets and requests as a guide.

DAY 229

Worship

Get alone with God. Find a quiet place. Sit down. Silence all distractions.

Scripture: Jeremiah ㉟ ㊱ ㊲

In today's reading, notice how God uses Jeremiah to re-write the scrolls that were burned by Jehoiakim. What you'll notice in verse 32, is that "this time, [Jeremiah] added much more!" to what was first written. This is a great illustration that shows us God's role as a redeemer. He restores broken and lost things into His glory.

Prayer

What is God saying to you? What do you need to say to God? Use a prayer model and your monthly prayer targets and requests as a guide.

DAY 230

Worship

Get alone with God. Find a quiet place. Sit down. Silence all distractions.

Scripture: Jeremiah ㊳ ㊴ ㊵   Psalm ㊲ ㊲

In today's reading, it finally happens. Jerusalem falls. Despite Jeremiah's praying and plies against it, God's plan prevailed. This hints at another aspect of God's character. He's consistent, and His plan always comes to pass. Even we think we've made a dent in God's plan, He's still in control!

Prayer

What is God saying to you? What do you need to say to God? Use a prayer model and your monthly prayer targets and requests as a guide.

DAY 231

Worship

Get alone with God. Find a quiet place. Sit down. Silence all distractions.

Scripture: 2 Kings (24) (25)   2 Chronicles (36)

In today's reading, God begins the process of restoring Jerusalem. God speaks through King Cyrus and says, "Any of you who are his people may go there for this task. And may the Lord your God be with you!" It's in these verses that God begins planting the seeds for Judah to be restored. But in order for God to move, it takes people who are devoted to him.

Prayer

What is God saying to you? What do you need to say to God? Use a prayer model and your monthly prayer targets and requests as a guide.

COMMUNITY

I attended a church service this week (circle):   YES   NO

I shared my faith and talked about my church with others this week (circle):   YES   NO

I connected with other Christians in a smaller group this week. If yes, describe.

DAY 232

Worship
Get alone with God. Find a quiet place. Sit down. Silence all distractions.

Scripture: Habakkuk ① ② ③
As you read today, notice God's response to Habakkuk in chapter 1. God says to him, "For I am doing something in your own day, something you wouldn't believe even if someone told you about it." Though Habakkuk doesn't see it, God is actually doing something in the greater story. When we're able to zoom out of our own circumstances, we can see the bigger picture of God's plan.

Prayer
What is God saying to you? What do you need to say to God? Use a prayer model and your monthly prayer targets and requests as a guide.

DAY 233

Worship
Get alone with God. Find a quiet place. Sit down. Silence all distractions.

Scripture: Jeremiah ㊶ ㊷ ㊸ ㊹ ㊺
For today's reading, God makes it clear that the punishment for sin is death. This is why God's plan is to destroy Jerusalem. But as you read today, remember that your sin is the same: it deserves death! However, your death was paid by Jesus on the cross. His death covers the punishment of our sins so that we can live free of guilt and shame.

Prayer
What is God saying to you? What do you need to say to God? Use a prayer model and your monthly prayer targets and requests as a guide.

DAY 234

Worship
Get alone with God. Find a quiet place. Sit down. Silence all distractions.

Scripture: Jeremiah (46) (47) (48)
In today's reading, God sends a message concerning Moab. Though they haven't experienced many trials or tribulations, Moab still deals with idolatry and sin. However, their idols are not golden statues: it's their wealth. Idolatry can look all sorts of ways, but at the end of the day, God wants to be the source of our strength and stability.

Prayer
What is God saying to you? What do you need to say to God? Use a prayer model and your monthly prayer targets and requests as a guide.

DAY 235

Worship
Get alone with God. Find a quiet place. Sit down. Silence all distractions.

Scripture: Jeremiah (49) (50)
As you read today, try to remember the illustration that is given in chapter 50: "My people have been lost sheep. Their shepherds have led them astray and turned them loose in the mountains." This illustration has appeared in earlier scriptures and will come up again later in the New Testament. This metaphor appears constantly. Remember that the Lord is our true shepherd: our true north.

Prayer
What is God saying to you? What do you need to say to God? Use a prayer model and your monthly prayer targets and requests as a guide.

DAY 236

Worship

Get alone with God. Find a quiet place. Sit down. Silence all distractions.

Scripture: Jeremiah (51) (52)

In today's reading, you'll read more on the destruction of Babylon. But towards the end of the reading, God's provision can be seen in how He honors King Jehoiachin. Jehoiachin's obedience is noticed by God, and He provides for his every need. This is His posture towards us: when we steward what God gives us and choose to be obedient, God will honor it!

Prayer

What is God saying to you? What do you need to say to God? Use a prayer model and your monthly prayer targets and requests as a guide.

DAY 237

Worship

Get alone with God. Find a quiet place. Sit down. Silence all distractions.

Scripture: Lamentations (1) (2)

As you begin reading in Lamentations today, consider this new perspective on the sinfulness of Jerusalem: They never considered the future that would take place as a result of their sin. Perhaps if they listened to God and had thought about the repercussions of their sinful ways, they might have chosen a different path.

Prayer

What is God saying to you? What do you need to say to God? Use a prayer model and your monthly prayer targets and requests as a guide.

DAY 238

Worship
Get alone with God. Find a quiet place. Sit down. Silence all distractions.

Scripture: Lamentations ③ ④ ⑤
In today's reading, notice how the heart of the author shifts in chapter 5. Instead of complaining about what God did in Jerusalem, the attitude moves towards the action of repentance. This will be a great example to each of us: When there's sin in our lives, the best thing we can do is repent and turn our focus back to God.

Prayer
What is God saying to you? What do you need to say to God? Use a prayer model and your monthly prayer targets and requests as a guide.

COMMUNITY

I attended a church service this week (circle):   YES   NO

I shared my faith and talked about my church with others this week (circle):   YES   NO

I connected with other Christians in a smaller group this week.
If yes, describe.

DAY 239

Worship
Get alone with God. Find a quiet place. Sit down. Silence all distractions.

Scripture: Ezekiel ① ② ③ ④
As you begin reading in Ezekiel, chapter 3 may stick out to you. What God says to Ezekiel about His message is truly profound: Son of man, let all my words sink deep into your own heart first. What God might show you in this small verse is that His Word isn't meant to be strictly head-knowledge: it's meant to penetrate our hearts and change us from the inside out.

Prayer
What is God saying to you? What do you need to say to God? Use a prayer model and your monthly prayer targets and requests as a guide.

DAY 240

Worship
Get alone with God. Find a quiet place. Sit down. Silence all distractions.

Scripture: Ezekiel ⑤ ⑥ ⑦ ⑧
In today's reading, you might notice that the phrase "they shall know that I am the Lord" appears several times. This constant reminder is significant to us because it clearly shows us what God really wants: for us to know Him. He wants to be heard, acknowledged, and allowed to speak into your life.

Prayer
What is God saying to you? What do you need to say to God? Use a prayer model and your monthly prayer targets and requests as a guide.

DAY 241

Worship
Get alone with God. Find a quiet place. Sit down. Silence all distractions.

Scripture: Ezekiel (9) (10) (11) (12)
As you read today, take a moment to reflect on how God has been so patient with you. Just as he was with the people of Judah, God's mercies are new every morning, and he always believes the best for us. His faithfulness will never fail!

Prayer
What is God saying to you? What do you need to say to God? Use a prayer model and your monthly prayer targets and requests as a guide.

DAY 242

Worship
Get alone with God. Find a quiet place. Sit down. Silence all distractions.

Scripture: Ezekiel (13) (14) (15)
As you read today, let the words on the page remind you of God's character. He addresses the issue of false prophets, magicians, and sorcerers to remind the people that He is the source of true power. He is all-powerful, and wickedness will never thwart God's plan for His family.

Prayer
What is God saying to you? What do you need to say to God? Use a prayer model and your monthly prayer targets and requests as a guide.

DAY 243

Worship

Get alone with God. Find a quiet place. Sit down. Silence all distractions.

Scripture: Ezekiel (16) (17)

In your reading today, God continues to return back to the idea of a "broken covenant." Let this show you that God's focus was always on the relationship between Him and the Israelites. God wants a real, intimate connection with you!

Prayer

What is God saying to you? What do you need to say to God? Use a prayer model and your monthly prayer targets and requests as a guide.

DAY 244

Worship

Get alone with God. Find a quiet place. Sit down. Silence all distractions.

Scripture: Ezekiel (18) (19) (20)

As you read today, notice the grace that God continues to extend to the people of Israel. Even when they ignore God and disobey Him, his grace keeps coming. In the end, their sins deserve justice. But God's grace never runs out.

Prayer

What is God saying to you? What do you need to say to God? Use a prayer model and your monthly prayer targets and requests as a guide.

DAY 245

Worship

Get alone with God. Find a quiet place. Sit down. Silence all distractions.

Scripture: Ezekiel ㉑ ㉒

In today's reading, God is getting ready to act on Israel by unleashing His wrath on them for their sin. This reminds us that God is the exact opposite of sin. God and sin cannot coexist in the same space, like darkness can't occupy the same space as light. Allow God into your life to restore and bring joy into it.

Prayer

What is God saying to you? What do you need to say to God? Use a prayer model and your monthly prayer targets and requests as a guide.

COMMUNITY

I attended a church service this week (circle):   YES   NO

I shared my faith and talked about my church with others this week (circle):   YES   NO

I connected with other Christians in a smaller group this week.
If yes, describe.

DAY 246

Worship

Get alone with God. Find a quiet place. Sit down. Silence all distractions.

Scripture: Ezekiel ㉓ ㉔

As you read today, even though you're in the Old Testament, think about how Jesus is pictured through Ezekiel losing his wife before Judah's destructions. God does this to Ezekiel so that he would understand the cost of sin. God sent Jesus to pay for our sin, as fully God and fully man, so that he could feel the pain of our sins. What a powerful picture of His mercy!

Prayer

What is God saying to you? What do you need to say to God? Use a prayer model and your monthly prayer targets and requests as a guide.

DAY 247

Worship

Get alone with God. Find a quiet place. Sit down. Silence all distractions.

Scripture: Ezekiel ㉕ ㉖ ㉗

In today's reading, you'll mostly be covering the destruction of several cities including Ammon, Moab, Edom, Philistia, and Tyre. Notice how God's words are coming to pass. What has been prophesied, spoken of, and commanded is coming to pass in these books. While what's happening here may seem harsh, it's actually a great reminder to us that God is faithful!

Prayer

What is God saying to you? What do you need to say to God? Use a prayer model and your monthly prayer targets and requests as a guide.

DAY 248

Worship

Get alone with God. Find a quiet place. Sit down. Silence all distractions.

Scripture: Ezekiel (28) (29) (30)

As you continue reading about what God is doing in Tyre, Sidon, and Israel, remember that God is good, just, and the source of all true strength. Judah spent more time finding sources for power and strength than they did seeking God. And in the end, God reveals his power and strength to the fullest.

Prayer

What is God saying to you? What do you need to say to God? Use a prayer model and your monthly prayer targets and requests as a guide.

DAY 249

Worship

Get alone with God. Find a quiet place. Sit down. Silence all distractions.

Scripture: Ezekiel (31) (32) (33)

In today's reading, there's an illustration in chapter 33 that may stand out to you. God compares Ezekiel to watchmen, who alert the city when an enemy is coming. If the city ignores the alert, the attack and the consequences are theirs to be responsible for. What God shows us is that we are responsible for our own obedience to Him as believers, not for how others respond to him.

Prayer

What is God saying to you? What do you need to say to God? Use a prayer model and your monthly prayer targets and requests as a guide.

DAY 250

Worship
Get alone with God. Find a quiet place. Sit down. Silence all distractions.

Scripture: Ezekiel (34) (35) (36)
As you read today, notice God's integrity in His actions. Edom receives the destruction they've deserved, and God isn't holding back who He is to them at all. He is the only one we can truly depend on to be the same yesterday, today, and forever.

Prayer
What is God saying to you? What do you need to say to God? Use a prayer model and your monthly prayer targets and requests as a guide.

DAY 251

Worship
Get alone with God. Find a quiet place. Sit down. Silence all distractions.

Scripture: Ezekiel (37) (38) (39)
In today's reading, you might see the phrase "in latter days' appear a few times in chapter 38. Most scholars believe that what's being prophesied is actually meant to happen in the end times. God is always in the moment, and yet, always outside of time and thinking beyond the present.

Prayer
What is God saying to you? What do you need to say to God? Use a prayer model and your monthly prayer targets and requests as a guide.

DAY 252

Worship
Get alone with God. Find a quiet place. Sit down. Silence all distractions.

Scripture: Ezekiel (40) (41) (42)
In today's reading, God speaks to Ezekiel about the new Temple that will be built. What's interesting in this passage is that the walls being built are not meant for defense; In fact, they're almost designed to allow people in, rather than keep people out! This shows us that God wants to be inviting, open, and available to us!

Prayer
What is God saying to you? What do you need to say to God? Use a prayer model and your monthly prayer targets and requests as a guide.

COMMUNITY

I attended a church service this week (circle):   YES   NO

I shared my faith and talked about my church with others this week (circle):   YES   NO

I connected with other Christians in a smaller group this week.
If yes, describe.

DAY 253

Worship
Get alone with God. Find a quiet place. Sit down. Silence all distractions.

Scripture: Ezekiel (43) (44) (45)
In all of the reading you've done so far, you may have noticed that God's standards for His people have gotten more and more rigid. This is not because God wanted to establish a host of impossible requirements for His people that would last until the end of time. But rather, this is so that the people would realize their need for a Savior: someone to come in and fulfill the law for them and establish a new kind of kingdom.

Prayer
What is God saying to you? What do you need to say to God? Use a prayer model and your monthly prayer targets and requests as a guide.

DAY 254

Worship
Get alone with God. Find a quiet place. Sit down. Silence all distractions.

Scripture: Ezekiel (46) (47) (48)
In today's reading, God gives His instructions to the Hebrew people. One important detail to note is that they are required to enter and exit through different gates at feasts and festivals. This is a cultural symbol for them, almost meaning that they can never go back from where they came. For you, this means that when you decide to repent and turn to God, you will never be the same.

Prayer
What is God saying to you? What do you need to say to God? Use a prayer model and your monthly prayer targets and requests as a guide.

DAY 255

Worship

Get alone with God. Find a quiet place. Sit down. Silence all distractions.

Scripture: Joel ① ② ③

Today, you will begin a new book: the book of Joel! As you read, you may notice that Joel is very well-versed in scripture! This is why he's able to speak into Israel's situation and give them hope. This is powerful for you and I; When we read scripture, it shows us more about who God is and gives us hope!

Prayer

What is God saying to you? What do you need to say to God? Use a prayer model and your monthly prayer targets and requests as a guide.

DAY 256

Worship

Get alone with God. Find a quiet place. Sit down. Silence all distractions.

Scripture: Daniel ① ② ③

In today's reading, it's another new book! As you read, look at how God is a provider for Daniel. When he needs wisdom, God delivers. When his leaders need compassionate hearts, God makes a way. God is a provider for those who trust in him!

Prayer

What is God saying to you? What do you need to say to God? Use a prayer model and your monthly prayer targets and requests as a guide.

DAY 257

Worship

Get alone with God. Find a quiet place. Sit down. Silence all distractions.

Scripture: Daniel ④ ⑤ ⑥

In today's reading, you will read about Daniel in the lion's den: a classic story most of us are familiar with! God's provision is seen again in this scene with Daniel in the den. In fact, Darius sees God's angel protecting Daniel, and Darius decides to instead throw in the people who caught Daniel in the first place. God's provision never fails for those who worship and put their trust in God!

Prayer

What is God saying to you? What do you need to say to God? Use a prayer model and your monthly prayer targets and requests as a guide.

DAY 258

Worship

Get alone with God. Find a quiet place. Sit down. Silence all distractions.

Scripture: Daniel ⑦ ⑧ ⑨

As you read today, you may notice that the book of Daniel shifts from hope literature into "end times" prophesy. This shows us that God is never existing only in our current moment. In fact, God is omniscient: outside of time and holding unlimited power.

Prayer

What is God saying to you? What do you need to say to God? Use a prayer model and your monthly prayer targets and requests as a guide.

DAY 259

Worship
Get alone with God. Find a quiet place. Sit down. Silence all distractions.

Scripture: Daniel (10) (11) (12)
In today's reading, you will read about Daniel in the lion's den: a classic story most of us are familiar with! God's provision is seen again in this scene with Daniel in the den. In fact, Darius sees God's angel protecting Daniel, and Darius decides to instead throw in the people who caught Daniel in the first place. God's provision never fails for those who worship and put their trust in God!

Prayer
What is God saying to you? What do you need to say to God? Use a prayer model and your monthly prayer targets and requests as a guide.

COMMUNITY

I attended a church service this week (circle):   YES   NO

I shared my faith and talked about my church with others this week (circle):   YES   NO

I connected with other Christians in a smaller group this week.
If yes, describe.

DAY 260

Worship

Get alone with God. Find a quiet place. Sit down. Silence all distractions.

Scripture: Ezra (1) (2) (3)

Today you begin the book of Ezra! As you read its first few chapters, notice the word "freewill" appear when talking about offerings. Not only does this lay the groundwork for what we call today, "tithe and offering", but it also shows us an aspect of God's character. He doesn't just want us to worship him because we have to, but because we want to!

Prayer

What is God saying to you? What do you need to say to God? Use a prayer model and your monthly prayer targets and requests as a guide.

DAY 261

Worship

Get alone with God. Find a quiet place. Sit down. Silence all distractions.

Scripture: Ezra (4) (5) (6)   Psalm (137)

As you read today, it's important to see that the Passover celebration mentioned in chapter 6 is open to all people! This is important because it used to be that Passover was an exclusive gathering. This slight attendance change shows us that at this point in time, God is making himself more available to be worshiped and known.

Prayer

What is God saying to you? What do you need to say to God? Use a prayer model and your monthly prayer targets and requests as a guide.

DAY 262

Worship
Get alone with God. Find a quiet place. Sit down. Silence all distractions.

Scripture: Haggai ① ②
As you read today, you begin another new book: Haggai. He brings up an interesting point in chapter 2 that God has been driving for a good portion of the Old Testament. Unclean hearts can't produce clean things. That is why God was to purify us from the inside out so that we can glorify Him and do His good works.

Prayer
What is God saying to you? What do you need to say to God? Use a prayer model and your monthly prayer targets and requests as a guide.

DAY 263

Worship
Get alone with God. Find a quiet place. Sit down. Silence all distractions.

Scripture: Zechariah ① ② ③ ④
In today's reading, notice how Zechariah got to where he is. He's only alive to spread the truth about what God had done to the current generations' ancestors. This shows us that God's truth stands the test of time, and that God will never change!

Prayer
What is God saying to you? What do you need to say to God? Use a prayer model and your monthly prayer targets and requests as a guide.

DAY 264

Worship

Get alone with God. Find a quiet place. Sit down. Silence all distractions.

Scripture: Zechariah ⑤ ⑥ ⑦ ⑧ ⑨

As you read today, don't get too lost in the dreams, visions, and prophecies. Remember, each verse and chapter is part of the greater story God is writing. This story is about Jesus coming to the earth to right every wrong in order to restore God's family.

Prayer

What is God saying to you? What do you need to say to God? Use a prayer model and your monthly prayer targets and requests as a guide.

DAY 265

Worship

Get alone with God. Find a quiet place. Sit down. Silence all distractions.

Scripture: Zechariah ⑩ ⑪ ⑫ ⑬ ⑭

In today's reading, we see another direct prophecy of Jesus in chapter 12. It says in verse 10, "They will look on me whom they have pierced and mourn for him as for an only son." This shows us that God is dropping small pieces of hope throughout scripture for what is to come: the ultimate super-weapon against the Enemy, Jesus!

Prayer

What is God saying to you? What do you need to say to God? Use a prayer model and your monthly prayer targets and requests as a guide.

DAY 266

Worship
Get alone with God. Find a quiet place. Sit down. Silence all distractions.

Scripture: Esther ① ② ③ ④ ⑤
Today we begin Esther, the only book in all of scripture that doesn't directly mention God's name. However, we see him in the shadows all throughout this book. What a great reminder for us, that even when we feel like we are alone God is still present and working when we cannot see him!

Prayer
What is God saying to you? What do you need to say to God? Use a prayer model and your monthly prayer targets and requests as a guide.

COMMUNITY

I attended a church service this week (circle):   YES   NO

I shared my faith and talked about my church with others this week (circle):   YES   NO

I connected with other Christians in a smaller group this week.
If yes, describe.

DAY 267

Get alone with God. Find a quiet place. Sit down. Silence all distractions.

Scripture: Esther ⑥ ⑦ ⑧ ⑨ ⑩
As you read today, don't forget that what you may perceive as God's absence is actually His sovereignty. God is so powerful and personal that He doesn't need the spotlight to be seen and to act. God can work with a minor drunken fool just as much as He can with a major flood!

Prayer
What is God saying to you? What do you need to say to God? Use a prayer model and your monthly prayer targets and requests as a guide.

DAY 268

Worship
Get alone with God. Find a quiet place. Sit down. Silence all distractions.

Scripture: Ezra ⑦ ⑧ ⑨ ⑩
In today's reading, we get another reminder that it's always wisest to consult with God before making big decisions. When it had to do with the relationship between the people of Jerusalem and the pagans, Ezra somewhat "rolled with the punches" and followed the people. However, we should always allow God into our circumstances!

Prayer
What is God saying to you? What do you need to say to God? Use a prayer model and your monthly prayer targets and requests as a guide.

DAY 269

Worship

Get alone with God. Find a quiet place. Sit down. Silence all distractions.

Scripture: Nehemiah ① ② ③ ④ ⑤

As you ready today, we see that Nehemiah follows through with what we talked about yesterday. He seeks God and asks for direction on how to serve Him. Nehemiah has the clarity he needs because of this decision to consult with God first!

Prayer

What is God saying to you? What do you need to say to God? Use a prayer model and your monthly prayer targets and requests as a guide.

DAY 270

Worship

Get alone with God. Find a quiet place. Sit down. Silence all distractions.

Scripture: Nehemiah ⑥ ⑦

As you ready today, notice what happens with Nehemiah in chapter 6. Even though the wall is completed and God receives all of the glory, Nehemiah's personal life is falling through the cracks. It's possible to be doing everything right on the outside but not be truly following God on the inside. This is why God wants not just our actions to be righteous, but for our hearts to be devoted to Him.

Prayer

What is God saying to you? What do you need to say to God? Use a prayer model and your monthly prayer targets and requests as a guide.

DAY 271

Worship
Get alone with God. Find a quiet place. Sit down. Silence all distractions.

Scripture: Nehemiah (8) (9) (10)
In today's reading, we see that the exiles are practicing a sacred gathering in which they read the Word and remind themselves of God's faithfulness. This is exactly what the Word is meant to do for us: remind us of God's continued faithfulness and how he's working in our present.

Prayer
What is God saying to you? What do you need to say to God? Use a prayer model and your monthly prayer targets and requests as a guide.

DAY 272

Worship
Get alone with God. Find a quiet place. Sit down. Silence all distractions.

Scripture: Nehemiah (11) (12) (13)   Psalm (126)
In today's reading, we continue in Nehemiah's story. However, Psalm 126 reminds us that there are still things to be restored by God. Their hearts have to be completely made new to be new people, not just geographically move. God wants to change us, not outside-in, but inside-out.

Prayer
What is God saying to you? What do you need to say to God? Use a prayer model and your monthly prayer targets and requests as a guide.

DAY 273

Worship
Get alone with God. Find a quiet place. Sit down. Silence all distractions.

Scripture: Malachi ① ② ③ ④
As you read today, you'll see that we're entering the book of Malachi. Some passages can be a little confusing and contradicting to what we know about God's character. But remember, all scripture is interpreted through all scripture. God is consistent, so don't let individual verses twist your theology. Think back to what you know to be true about God and let that build your faith.

Prayer
What is God saying to you? What do you need to say to God? Use a prayer model and your monthly prayer targets and requests as a guide.

COMMUNITY

I attended a church service this week (circle):   YES   NO

I shared my faith and talked about my church with others this week (circle):   YES   NO

I connected with other Christians in a smaller group this week.
If yes, describe.

DAY 274

Worship
Get alone with God. Find a quiet place. Sit down. Silence all distractions.

Scripture: Luke (1)   John (1)
In these chapters, you'll see God's character is shown by how He keeps His word. He promises Zechariah and Elizabeth a son and lists off everything that He will do, and He promises Mary a child. When God clearly says He is going to do something, He will. He is faithful.

Prayer
What is God saying to you? What do you need to say to God? Use a prayer model and your monthly prayer targets and requests as a guide.

DAY 275

Worship
Get alone with God. Find a quiet place. Sit down. Silence all distractions.

Scripture: Matthew (1)   Luke (2)
As you know, God doesn't do anything on accident. There's purpose to everything He does. God chose Mary, an average woman, to give birth to, and raise Jesus. God wants to use you today and every day you have here on earth. Ask Him to show you His purpose for today.

Prayer
What is God saying to you? What do you need to say to God? Use a prayer model and your monthly prayer targets and requests as a guide.

DAY 276

Worship
Get alone with God. Find a quiet place. Sit down. Silence all distractions.

Scripture: Matthew ②
We can trust God because He is our Heavenly Father. Throughout today's reading, you'll see how God protects Joseph, Mary, Jesus, and the Wise Men from King Herod. Pay attention to how God protects them through preparation and obedience.

Prayer
What is God saying to you? What do you need to say to God? Use a prayer model and your monthly prayer targets and requests as a guide.

DAY 277

Worship
Get alone with God. Find a quiet place. Sit down. Silence all distractions.

Scripture: Matthew ③   Mark ①   Luke ③
It's evident by now that God is all about family. He places the lonely in family. You'll see in today's reading the different backgrounds our authors have while experiencing the same thing. Though all different in perspective, the truth remains the same. When you're read these scriptures, pay attention to how God uses their differences to unite the message of the Gospel.

Prayer
What is God saying to you? What do you need to say to God? Use a prayer model and your monthly prayer targets and requests as a guide.

DAY 278

Worship

Get alone with God. Find a quiet place. Sit down. Silence all distractions.

Scripture: Matthew ④   Luke ④ ⑤

Today's scriptures show us God's heart for the lost. Jesus connected with some of the most looked-over individuals by society's standards. You'll see today God is close to the brokenhearted, the sick, and all of us as sinners. His heart is to bring the lost back home to Him, where we all belong

Prayer

What is God saying to you? What do you need to say to God? Use a prayer model and your monthly prayer targets and requests as a guide.

DAY 279

Worship

Get alone with God. Find a quiet place. Sit down. Silence all distractions.

Scripture: John ② ③ ④

As you read today, focus on God's heart. Look for how He convicts and wants to draw His sons and daughters back to Him. There's nothing that can rival the love and hope we have in Jesus. Look for how He speaks to us through His word.

Prayer

What is God saying to you? What do you need to say to God? Use a prayer model and your monthly prayer targets and requests as a guide.

DAY 280

Worship
Get alone with God. Find a quiet place. Sit down. Silence all distractions.

Scripture: Matthew (8)   Mark (2)
In today's scriptures, you can see God's generosity through Jesus. When God is generous to us, it tends to spark generosity in us as well. After all, we are created in His image. If you are faithful and obedient to God, He will be generous. He is faithful!

Prayer
What is God saying to you? What do you need to say to God? Use a prayer model and your monthly prayer targets and requests as a guide.

COMMUNITY

I attended a church service this week (circle):   YES   NO

I shared my faith and talked about my church with others this week
(circle):   YES   NO

I connected with other Christians in a smaller group this week.
If yes, describe.

DAY 281

Worship
Get alone with God. Find a quiet place. Sit down. Silence all distractions.

Scripture: John (5)
We all experience struggles in life, and it's common to become defensive when we feel attacked. In today's chapter, we see the humility Jesus displayed. Humility comes at the price of allowing our pride to die. We want to take steps to live like Jesus did. Take note of how Jesus displayed humility while you read.

Prayer
What is God saying to you? What do you need to say to God? Use a prayer model and your monthly prayer targets and requests as a guide.

DAY 282

Worship
Get alone with God. Find a quiet place. Sit down. Silence all distractions.

Scripture: Matthew (12)   Mark (3)   Luke (6)
Today, we experience more of Jesus' gentleness, mercy, and healing, even in the midst of danger. Though Jesus is missional, He is still relational because He wants to let the Gentiles know that He is the Messiah and for them, which was uncommon knowledge for any Gentile. When it can all cost Him His life, He still pursues the mission of God.

Prayer
What is God saying to you? What do you need to say to God? Use a prayer model and your monthly prayer targets and requests as a guide.

DAY 283

Worship
Get alone with God. Find a quiet place. Sit down. Silence all distractions.

Scripture: Matthew (5) (6) (7)
The Beatitudes seem like an impossible checklist for us as Christians, but thankfully, Jesus fulfills everything He speaks. God shows His majesty and greatness throughout these scriptures. He wants to continually purify us as we engage and draw closer to Him.

Prayer
What is God saying to you? What do you need to say to God? Use a prayer model and your monthly prayer targets and requests as a guide.

DAY 284

Worship
Get alone with God. Find a quiet place. Sit down. Silence all distractions.

Scripture: Matthew (9)   Luke (7)
In these scriptures, a sinful woman comes to Jesus while He's eating dinner and starts washing His feet with her tears and putting perfume on them. She showed love and the awareness that she needed forgiveness for her sins. This shows that God wants a relationship with us, and for us to want Him just as much.

Prayer
What is God saying to you? What do you need to say to God? Use a prayer model and your monthly prayer targets and requests as a guide.

DAY 285

Worship

Get alone with God. Find a quiet place. Sit down. Silence all distractions.

Scripture: Matthew (11)

In today's reading, notice that there's something interesting about how God gives rest. You'll notice that it's not the same as the rest we imagine. Finding rest in God is doing His will the right way with Him alongside us. He takes what doesn't fit and positions us to grow in Him and spiritual family.

Prayer

What is God saying to you? What do you need to say to God? Use a prayer model and your monthly prayer targets and requests as a guide.

DAY 286

Worship

Get alone with God. Find a quiet place. Sit down. Silence all distractions.

Scripture: Luke (11)

In the beginning of this chapter, Jesus teaches the disciples how to pray. You can see God's desire for a relationship with us. Jesus explains to them that God wants an intimate relationship with us. He wants us to talk to Him about everything that happens in our lives, from the little things to the big things.

Prayer

What is God saying to you? What do you need to say to God? Use a prayer model and your monthly prayer targets and requests as a guide.

DAY 287

Worship
Get alone with God. Find a quiet place. Sit down. Silence all distractions.

Scripture: Matthew ⑬   Luke ⑧
It's amazing that God's heart is all about making sure that everybody from all walks of life can come to know and have a relationship with Him. God's heart towards everyone going through anything is the same. In today's reading, you'll see that He is no respecter of man. He doesn't treat one person differently from the next and doesn't discriminate.

Prayer
What is God saying to you? What do you need to say to God? Use a prayer model and your monthly prayer targets and requests as a guide.

COMMUNITY

I attended a church service this week (circle):   YES   NO

I shared my faith and talked about my church with others this week (circle):   YES   NO

I connected with other Christians in a smaller group this week.
If yes, describe.

DAY 288

Worship
Get alone with God. Find a quiet place. Sit down. Silence all distractions.

Scripture: Mark ④ ⑤
In today's reading, pay attention to how detailed and intentional Jesus is. From one miracle to another, Jesus wanted His disciples to have faith in Him, that they were going to be safe and make it through that storm. He keeps us safe and close to Him in our storms or battles when we keep Him close to our hearts.

Prayer
What is God saying to you? What do you need to say to God? Use a prayer model and your monthly prayer targets and requests as a guide.

DAY 289

Worship
Get alone with God. Find a quiet place. Sit down. Silence all distractions.

Scripture: Matthew ⑩
When you read today, remember God is faithful. In Matthew 10:39, Jesus says that "Whoever finds their life will lose it, and whoever loses their life for my sake will find it." This perfectly shows God's faithfulness to us as His children. If we stay faithful and surrender everything we have to Him, He will reward us because of it.

Prayer
What is God saying to you? What do you need to say to God? Use a prayer model and your monthly prayer targets and requests as a guide.

DAY 290

Worship
Get alone with God. Find a quiet place. Sit down. Silence all distractions.

Scripture: Matthew ⑭   Mark ⑥   Luke ⑨
In the scriptures today, you get to experience different perspectives again. It's the famous story of walking on water. In your day to day, you don't literally get to walk on water, but it paints a beautiful picture of what our faith can do when it's strong and when it's weak. It only takes seconds for it to waiver at times. What do you see on display today from God's character?

Prayer
What is God saying to you? What do you need to say to God? Use a prayer model and your monthly prayer targets and requests as a guide.

DAY 291

Worship
Get alone with God. Find a quiet place. Sit down. Silence all distractions.

Scripture: John ⑥
In the reading today, Jesus ends up losing a lot of His followers because they couldn't fathom what He meant and what He was saying. God wants us to understand and know His heart and His words, and He gave us one of the best tools to understand those things; the Bible! The Bible is a book all about God and His people and so many true stories and parables, and all of those things help us understand more of who He is. What an awesome gift!

Prayer
What is God saying to you? What do you need to say to God? Use a prayer model and your monthly prayer targets and requests as a guide.

DAY 292

Worship

Get alone with God. Find a quiet place. Sit down. Silence all distractions.

Scripture: Matthew (15)   Mark (7)

Today, we see God our Healer. Many times, when we think of healing, our minds go to a physical sickness, which God is able to heal. Not only does God want to heal our bodies, but He wants to heal our hearts, minds, and lives.

Prayer

What is God saying to you? What do you need to say to God? Use a prayer model and your monthly prayer targets and requests as a guide.

DAY 293

Worship

Get alone with God. Find a quiet place. Sit down. Silence all distractions.

Scripture: Matthew (16)   Mark (8)

As you begin reading today, remember that God has a plan and purpose to save all humanity, even when it doesn't make sense. You'll see that Jesus' love transcends any attitude that His disciples give Him, specifically Peter, in today's scriptures. He is preparing their hearts for His death, resurrection, and the aftermath of what is to come. When you read, think about how God is preparing you for what's to come.

Prayer

What is God saying to you? What do you need to say to God? Use a prayer model and your monthly prayer targets and requests as a guide.

DAY 294

Worship

Get alone with God. Find a quiet place. Sit down. Silence all distractions.

Scripture: Matthew (17)   Mark (9)

In the chapters today, you'll read when Jesus heals the demonized boy, but the focus is on the boy's father. The self-awareness of the father is pretty humbling when he says, "I believe. Help my unbelief!" God doesn't judge or condemn us when we ask Him to build our faith; He's glad we do and wants to grant us faith. All we have to do is ask!

Prayer

What is God saying to you? What do you need to say to God? Use a prayer model and your monthly prayer targets and requests as a guide.

COMMUNITY

I attended a church service this week (circle):   YES   NO

I shared my faith and talked about my church with others this week (circle):   YES   NO

I connected with other Christians in a smaller group this week.
If yes, describe.

DAY 295

Worship
Get alone with God. Find a quiet place. Sit down. Silence all distractions.

Scripture: Matthew (18)
In today's reading, you'll see how much God cares about relationships. We've all experienced offense, whether if it's being offended or offending someone. The enemy wants to cause division and distract us from what really matters and what Jesus is building, but Jesus gives us the tools we need to resolve relationships and move forward.

Prayer
What is God saying to you? What do you need to say to God? Use a prayer model and your monthly prayer targets and requests as a guide.

DAY 296

Worship
Get alone with God. Find a quiet place. Sit down. Silence all distractions.

Scripture: John (7) (8)
In these chapters, Jesus is teaching the Pharisees that He is the Light of the World, but they don't believe or understand because they don't know God the Father. Take note of Jesus' persistence to help them understand, sometimes harshly, even if they won't know what He's talking about until what He's saying comes to pass. As you read, pay attention to the patience and diligence Jesus displays.

Prayer
What is God saying to you? What do you need to say to God? Use a prayer model and your monthly prayer targets and requests as a guide.

DAY 297

Worship

Get alone with God. Find a quiet place. Sit down. Silence all distractions.

Scripture: John ⑨ ⑩

Just like any parent; God loves to see His children live in freedom. God places value on us as His creation. When you read today, see it with that in mind. There's nothing that cannot do and nothing that can stop His love for us!

Prayer

What is God saying to you? What do you need to say to God? Use a prayer model and your monthly prayer targets and requests as a guide.

DAY 298

Worship

Get alone with God. Find a quiet place. Sit down. Silence all distractions.

Scripture: Luke ⑩

Jesus is relatable, that's why God sent Him to earth. His humanity is a connection point for us to reference. Yes, He is fully God, but He is fully man. Experiencing life on the same level as us. You'll see that today when you read the story of the Good Samaritan. The Samaritan and Jesus have many things in common; look for it as you read!

Prayer

What is God saying to you? What do you need to say to God? Use a prayer model and your monthly prayer targets and requests as a guide.

DAY 299

Worship
Get alone with God. Find a quiet place. Sit down. Silence all distractions.

Scripture: Luke (12) (13)
God's judgment is different than society's judgment. It's never to leave you in fear and offense. As you'll see in today's reading, Peter and Paul encourage believers to check their hearts and continually seek the things that matter to God the most. God will take care of the rest because He is our Provider!

Prayer
What is God saying to you? What do you need to say to God? Use a prayer model and your monthly prayer targets and requests as a guide.

DAY 300

Worship
Get alone with God. Find a quiet place. Sit down. Silence all distractions.

Scripture: Luke (14) (15)
Today, we see God celebrating. As you read the parable of the lost son, this perfectly shows how God rejoices when we repent and ask Him into our hearts. We've always had a place in the family, but it's our decision to take part in it. We can easily allow thoughts of condemnation to sink in when we think about how sinful our lives are but remember that Jesus calls us clean! He sees our future in Him as our current reality.

Prayer
What is God saying to you? What do you need to say to God? Use a prayer model and your monthly prayer targets and requests as a guide.

DAY 301

Worship
Get alone with God. Find a quiet place. Sit down. Silence all distractions.

Scripture: Luke (16) (17)
Everything Jesus does is relational. Today, as you read, you'll see how He speaks to different crowds of people. He wants to meet them where they are. Ask God to speak to you where you're at today. Open and your heart and receive His word!

Prayer
What is God saying to you? What do you need to say to God? Use a prayer model and your monthly prayer targets and requests as a guide.

COMMUNITY

I attended a church service this week (circle):   YES   NO

I shared my faith and talked about my church with others this week (circle):   YES   NO

I connected with other Christians in a smaller group this week. If yes, describe.

DAY 302

Worship
Get alone with God. Find a quiet place. Sit down. Silence all distractions.

Scripture: John (11)
In this chapter, you'll read about Jesus raising Lazarus from the dead. When Jesus comes to Martha and Mary, and they show Jesus Lazarus' body, there is a verse that just says, "Jesus wept." This shows the empathy that God has towards us. What's important to us as His children is important to Him, like how Jesus was with Martha and Mary. When our hearts break, His heart breaks for us. He is our comforter, and He is there with us always.

Prayer
What is God saying to you? What do you need to say to God? Use a prayer model and your monthly prayer targets and requests as a guide.

DAY 303

Worship
Get alone with God. Find a quiet place. Sit down. Silence all distractions.

Scripture: Luke (18)
In this reading, Jesus talks to a ruler about how he can inherit eternal life. While this ruler was asking God what he can do to live eternally, Jesus truly knew his heart. He wasn't willing to give up everything he had to walk with him because he was still wanting to hold on to his wealth. As we keep reading God's word, we grow closer to His heart. As we stay committed to Him, we let go of things holding us back. This ruler wasn't ready, but the more we desire to know God, we can accept what He wants from us.

Prayer
What is God saying to you? What do you need to say to God? Use a prayer model and your monthly prayer targets and requests as a guide.

DAY 304

Worship
Get alone with God. Find a quiet place. Sit down. Silence all distractions.

Scripture: Matthew (19)   Mark (10)
Sometimes reading the Bible can be difficult. It can feel discouraging when we don't understand what it is saying. When that happens, just remember that you are in good company! God wants to walk with you step by step as you go through your journey as a Christian and reading His Word. Ask Him to give you the ears to hear and the eyes to see His heart and to know His Word.

Prayer
What is God saying to you? What do you need to say to God? Use a prayer model and your monthly prayer targets and requests as a guide.

DAY 305

Worship
Get alone with God. Find a quiet place. Sit down. Silence all distractions.

Scripture: Matthew (20) (21)
In today's reading, Jesus compares God's kingdom to vineyard workers. No matter what they do, they all get paid the same amount. This is shown to represent God's grace towards us. No matter who we are or what we do, He shows us all the same grace, and He gives it to us freely.

Prayer
What is God saying to you? What do you need to say to God? Use a prayer model and your monthly prayer targets and requests as a guide.

DAY 306

Worship
Get alone with God. Find a quiet place. Sit down. Silence all distractions.

Scripture: Luke (19)
In today's reading, one of the verses goes back to the foundation of why Jesus was on earth; "For the Son of Man came to seek and save the lost". This is a great reminder that God sent Jesus to find us where we're at and save us. God gives us the choice to follow Him and to live eternally. Thank God for that today!

Prayer
What is God saying to you? What do you need to say to God? Use a prayer model and your monthly prayer targets and requests as a guide.

DAY 307

Worship
Get alone with God. Find a quiet place. Sit down. Silence all distractions.

Scripture: Mark (11)   John (12)
In today's reading, we see moments of Jesus's humanity. At the end of John 12, there was a crowd of Greeks questioning Jesus on who He was. Some can say he was even troubled. But that never changed Jesus' faithfulness to us by dying on the cross. How do you see God's character and attributes in today's reading?

Prayer
What is God saying to you? What do you need to say to God? Use a prayer model and your monthly prayer targets and requests as a guide.

DAY 308

Worship
Get alone with God. Find a quiet place. Sit down. Silence all distractions.

Scripture: Matthew ㉒   Mark ⑫
In today's reading, be reminded of how precious you are to God! It can sometimes be easy to get caught up in wanting to do as much as possible for God's kingdom, and we should always have that posture of heart, but God loves anything that we do selflessly to build His kingdom!

Prayer
What is God saying to you? What do you need to say to God? Use a prayer model and your monthly prayer targets and requests as a guide.

COMMUNITY

I attended a church service this week (circle):   YES   NO

I shared my faith and talked about my church with others this week (circle):   YES   NO

I connected with other Christians in a smaller group this week.
If yes, describe.

DAY 309

Worship
Get alone with God. Find a quiet place. Sit down. Silence all distractions.

Scripture: Matthew (23)   Luke (20) (21)
In today's reading, specifically towards the end of Luke 21, Jesus talks about some of the signs of the end times. One part that really shows God's heart for us is when He talks about when we stand firm, we will not perish. That is one of the most reassuring things that we know! He will protect us, cover us, and make sure we are safe and saved so long as we stay firm in our faith!

Prayer
What is God saying to you? What do you need to say to God? Use a prayer model and your monthly prayer targets and requests as a guide.

DAY 310

Worship
Get alone with God. Find a quiet place. Sit down. Silence all distractions.

Scripture: Mark (13)
Today, take some time to thank God for the gift of eternal life. Reading about the end times for some people can be scary, and for others, it can be comforting. But no matter what, we are not alone, and Jesus promises life eternal with God. So take heart because we are part of an unstoppable kingdom!

Prayer
What is God saying to you? What do you need to say to God? Use a prayer model and your monthly prayer targets and requests as a guide.

DAY 311

Worship
Get alone with God. Find a quiet place. Sit down. Silence all distractions.

Scripture: Matthew 24
Jesus reminds us in today's reading to not be afraid and to "stay awake." This may be alarming, and it can feel like we don't know what to look for. Jesus reminds us that we will never know when the end times will be, but to stay faithful and obedient. We don't have to worry or concern ourselves about when this side of eternity is done. Be diligent in your faith and stay the course!

Prayer
What is God saying to you? What do you need to say to God? Use a prayer model and your monthly prayer targets and requests as a guide.

DAY 312

Worship
Get alone with God. Find a quiet place. Sit down. Silence all distractions.

Scripture: Matthew 25
Today, before you read, take a moment to think of everything God has done for you. A thankful heart and attitude can change your thinking instantly and transform the way you receive His word. Focus on His goodness and remind your heart who it belongs to.

Prayer
What is God saying to you? What do you need to say to God? Use a prayer model and your monthly prayer targets and requests as a guide.

DAY 313

Worship

Get alone with God. Find a quiet place. Sit down. Silence all distractions.

Scripture: Matthew (26)   Mark (14)

You'll see in today's reading that Jesus has a purpose to everything He does, even when we don't get why. We can try to figure out the intentions of Jesus, but it's best to know that the end result was to save all of humanity. Let's be thankful that we don't understand everything, but we serve a God who does.

Prayer

What is God saying to you? What do you need to say to God? Use a prayer model and your monthly prayer targets and requests as a guide.

DAY 314

Worship

Get alone with God. Find a quiet place. Sit down. Silence all distractions.

Scripture: Luke (22)   John (13)

While you read today, ask God to give perspective on how these moments must've felt for Jesus. Even though He is fully God, He is also fully man. There's something relatable about the realness of what was happening in these scriptures. Look for how God works in and through the situations.

Prayer

What is God saying to you? What do you need to say to God? Use a prayer model and your monthly prayer targets and requests as a guide.

DAY 315

Worship

Get alone with God. Find a quiet place. Sit down. Silence all distractions.

Scripture: John (14) (15) (16) (17)

Today, you'll notice a familiar theme throughout these chapters. Here's a couple of questions to ask yourself while reading. Why do you think Jesus is repetitive with these themes? How will you apply this to your life today?

Prayer

What is God saying to you? What do you need to say to God? Use a prayer model and your monthly prayer targets and requests as a guide.

COMMUNITY

I attended a church service this week (circle):   YES   NO

I shared my faith and talked about my church with others this week (circle):   YES   NO

I connected with other Christians in a smaller group this week.
If yes, describe.

DAY 316

Worship
Get alone with God. Find a quiet place. Sit down. Silence all distractions.

Scripture: Matthew ㉗   Mark ⑮

It's easy to read today's scriptures and think to yourself, "I would have never done that to Jesus." When you really take a moment and think about it, our sin is what brought Jesus to that very moment. Keep this in mind while reading; have you ever been wrongfully accused of something? How would your reaction compare to Jesus' response?

Prayer
What is God saying to you? What do you need to say to God? Use a prayer model and your monthly prayer targets and requests as a guide.

DAY 317

Worship
Get alone with God. Find a quiet place. Sit down. Silence all distractions.

Scripture: Luke ㉓   John ⑱ ⑲

Today's reading is the moment that changed history forever. When you unpack these scriptures, take time to soak in the story all over again. This is our salvation and where true life begins. Thank God for Jesus. Thank Jesus for The Holy Spirit. Thank The Holy Spirit for dwelling within you.

Prayer
What is God saying to you? What do you need to say to God? Use a prayer model and your monthly prayer targets and requests as a guide.

DAY 318

Worship

Get alone with God. Find a quiet place. Sit down. Silence all distractions.

Scripture: Matthew (28)   Mark (16)

In today's reading, we see Jesus has risen from the tomb. He is alive and better than ever, almost like He was never gone. This is where you'll see forgiveness, generosity, and mercy displayed over and over. Let these scriptures remind you of the countless times Jesus did the same for you.

Prayer

What is God saying to you? What do you need to say to God? Use a prayer model and your monthly prayer targets and requests as a guide.

DAY 319

Worship

Get alone with God. Find a quiet place. Sit down. Silence all distractions.

Scripture: Luke (24)   John (20) (21)

God never leaves us without, but we see throughout scripture that we cannot live without Him. You'll see Jesus preparing the disciples today for when He is gone. Pay attention to how He prepares and how He speaks with them. Think about how God prepares you for what's to come.

Prayer

What is God saying to you? What do you need to say to God? Use a prayer model and your monthly prayer targets and requests as a guide.

DAY 320

Worship
Get alone with God. Find a quiet place. Sit down. Silence all distractions.

Scripture: Acts (1)(2)(3)
In today's reading, you'll get to experience The Holy Spirit and the birth of the local church. This is so exciting, because you can see God's redemption and love for His creation throughout these chapters. What God says He will do, He does.

Prayer
What is God saying to you? What do you need to say to God? Use a prayer model and your monthly prayer targets and requests as a guide.

DAY 321

Worship
Get alone with God. Find a quiet place. Sit down. Silence all distractions.

Scripture: Acts (4)(5)(6)
People often say Christianity is too exclusive, but the gospel isn't exclusive; it's just specific. As you read today, look for specifics of our Christian faith and why the name of Jesus is significant.

Prayer
What is God saying to you? What do you need to say to God? Use a prayer model and your monthly prayer targets and requests as a guide.

DAY 322

Worship
Get alone with God. Find a quiet place. Sit down. Silence all distractions.

Scripture: Acts (7) (8)
In life, it can look and feel like the enemy has the upper hand. You'll see that in today's reading but pay close attention to what God is doing in the background. Look for God's sovereignty.

Prayer
What is God saying to you? What do you need to say to God? Use a prayer model and your monthly prayer targets and requests as a guide.

COMMUNITY

I attended a church service this week (circle):   YES   NO

I shared my faith and talked about my church with others this week (circle):   YES   NO

I connected with other Christians in a smaller group this week.
If yes, describe.

DAY 323

Worship
Get alone with God. Find a quiet place. Sit down. Silence all distractions.

Scripture: Acts (9) (10)
Do you know someone who desperately needs Jesus? Then today's reading should encourage you, even though it may not seem exciting. Look for it, because God will show you that He pursues those He loves.

Prayer
What is God saying to you? What do you need to say to God? Use a prayer model and your monthly prayer targets and requests as a guide.

DAY 324

Worship
Get alone with God. Find a quiet place. Sit down. Silence all distractions.

Scripture: Acts (11) (12)
There's quite a bit of back and forth with persecution in what we've been reading, but have you noticed something about those who stay obedient and faithful to what Jesus exemplified? Ask God to show you that today as you read.

Prayer
What is God saying to you? What do you need to say to God? Use a prayer model and your monthly prayer targets and requests as a guide.

DAY 325

Worship
Get alone with God. Find a quiet place. Sit down. Silence all distractions.

Scripture: Acts (13) (14)
It's no surprise by now that God makes Himself known. No matter what level of faith we have, He is always faithful. In every season of life, He provides. In today's reading, you'll see how generous and kind He is even as nations choose to live in disobedience.

Talk To God
What is God saying to you? What do you need to say to God? Use your monthly prayer targets to guide your conversation with Him.

DAY 326

Worship
Get alone with God. Find a quiet place. Sit down. Silence all distractions.

Scripture: James (1) (2) (3) (4) (5)
While reading the book of James today, it can become easy to get down on yourself, but that's not the purpose of this book. Allow God to speak to you and encourage you through James' words. It's good to know that even generations before us were just as human as we are.

Prayer
What is God saying to you? What do you need to say to God? Use a prayer model and your monthly prayer targets and requests as a guide.

DAY 327

Worship
Get alone with God. Find a quiet place. Sit down. Silence all distractions.

Scripture: Acts (15) (16)
Today, you'll catch another glimpse of God's love for us. You'll notice similar themes throughout today's reading of people trying to push old laws and attempting to exclude the Gentiles. God wants our hearts and our faith.

Prayer
What is God saying to you? What do you need to say to God? Use a prayer model and your monthly prayer targets and requests as a guide.

DAY 328

Worship
Get alone with God. Find a quiet place. Sit down. Silence all distractions.

Scripture: Galatians (1) (2) (3)
This is the first of Paul's letters to churches, and it's to a church he planted on his first missionary journey. You'll see in today's reading that God is all inclusive and Paul relays that to everyone in the letter. Because of Jesus' sacrifice for us, everyone is included into the spiritual family.

Prayer
What is God saying to you? What do you need to say to God? Use a prayer model and your monthly prayer targets and requests as a guide.

DAY 329

Worship
Get alone with God. Find a quiet place. Sit down. Silence all distractions.

Scripture: Galatians ④ ⑤ ⑥
As you read today, you can see God's generosity over and over again. Not only are we fellow heirs with Christ, but He gives us the Holy Spirit to bear fruit that honors Him. Take note of the other ways God is generous throughout your reading.

Prayer
What is God saying to you? What do you need to say to God? Use a prayer model and your monthly prayer targets and requests as a guide.

COMMUNITY

I attended a church service this week (circle):   YES   NO

I shared my faith and talked about my church with others this week (circle):   YES   NO

I connected with other Christians in a smaller group this week.
If yes, describe.

DAY 330

Worship

Get alone with God. Find a quiet place. Sit down. Silence all distractions.

Scripture: Acts (17)

Focus in on God's truth today while you read. You'll see that Paul testifies about Jesus, and they don't just take his word as fact; they crack open their scrolls every day. All truth comes from God; all else is opinion. Ask God to reveal His truth to you today.

Prayer

What is God saying to you? What do you need to say to God? Use a prayer model and your monthly prayer targets and requests as a guide.

DAY 331

Worship

Get alone with God. Find a quiet place. Sit down. Silence all distractions.

Scripture: 1 Thessalonians (1) (2) (3) (4) (5)   2 Thessalonians (1) (2) (3)

As you go into today's reading, look for God's character and attributes. See how Paul doesn't credit himself or others for the work that God is doing in and through the people of Thessalonica.

Prayer

What is God saying to you? What do you need to say to God? Use a prayer model and your monthly prayer targets and requests as a guide.

DAY 332

Worship
Get alone with God. Find a quiet place. Sit down. Silence all distractions.

Scripture: Acts ⑱ ⑲
In today's reading, you'll see how God is sovereign over timing and every detail. You'll see His hand at work in every detail and where the start of the gospel being spread into Asia. God is in the details, and every single one matters.

Prayer
What is God saying to you? What do you need to say to God? Use a prayer model and your monthly prayer targets and requests as a guide.

DAY 333

Worship
Get alone with God. Find a quiet place. Sit down. Silence all distractions.

Scripture: 1 Corinthians ① ② ③ ④
You can see in today's reading that Paul is helping the church of Corinth refocus their attention on what really matters. It's not about what our preferences are, but about the truth of God, what He has done and will do. Take time to write down what God is speaking to you about who He is through these scriptures.

Prayer
What is God saying to you? What do you need to say to God? Use a prayer model and your monthly prayer targets and requests as a guide.

DAY 334

Worship
Get alone with God. Find a quiet place. Sit down. Silence all distractions.

Scripture: 1 Corinthians ⑤ ⑥ ⑦ ⑧
Keeping an open heart and hands is key when it comes to everything God has for you. When you read today, it can seem like a ton of rules and judgment, but what you're seeing is God's way of keeping us focused on Him. The enemy wants nothing more than to distract and destroy you.

Prayer
What is God saying to you? What do you need to say to God? Use a prayer model and your monthly prayer targets and requests as a guide.

DAY 335

Worship
Get alone with God. Find a quiet place. Sit down. Silence all distractions.

Scripture: 1 Corinthians ⑨ ⑩ ⑪
Freedom in Christ does not give us the license to freely sin. It means we have and can find freedom from the sin that tempts us. God wants to reveal Himself to you more and more through reading His word and through the Holy Spirit.

Prayer
What is God saying to you? What do you need to say to God? Use a prayer model and your monthly prayer targets and requests as a guide.

DAY 336

Worship
Get alone with God. Find a quiet place. Sit down. Silence all distractions.

Scripture: 1 Corinthians (12) (13) (14)
With all of the personality tests and assessments that are made available to us today, it's easy to confuse them with the gifts that God has given us. The Spirit gives us gifts, and without Him, it means nothing and serves no purpose. In today's reading, God's generosity and love is on display. Take it in and ask Him to speak to you today!

Prayer
What is God saying to you? What do you need to say to God? Use a prayer model and your monthly prayer targets and requests as a guide.

COMMUNITY

I attended a church service this week (circle):   YES   NO

I shared my faith and talked about my church with others this week (circle):   YES   NO

I connected with other Christians in a smaller group this week.
If yes, describe.

DAY 337

Worship
Get alone with God. Find a quiet place. Sit down. Silence all distractions.

Scripture: 1 Corinthians (15) (16)
Today, we witness God's mercy in a huge way. Paul recognizes that he doesn't deserve everything God done for him; given his past. God is sovereign and will use whomever He wants to get the job done. Plus, it's amazing that God uses Paul to build the very thing Paul was determined to destroy.

Prayer
What is God saying to you? What do you need to say to God? Use a prayer model and your monthly prayer targets and requests as a guide.

DAY 338

Worship
Get alone with God. Find a quiet place. Sit down. Silence all distractions.

Scripture: 2 Corinthians (1) (2) (3) (4)
Paul reminds us in today's reading that God wants us to stay focused on Him. God doesn't need us, but He wants us. Not only does He want us, but He wants to live in us. Isn't that encouraging? Today, as you dive in, remember that truth!

Prayer
What is God saying to you? What do you need to say to God? Use a prayer model and your monthly prayer targets and requests as a guide.

DAY 339

Worship
Get alone with God. Find a quiet place. Sit down. Silence all distractions.

Scripture: 2 Corinthians (5) (6) (7) (8) (9)
We all face troubles and hard times; it's something that we see in the Bible over and over. We can't escape them, but we can find refuge in God. He is our strength, shield, and strong tower in time of need. Through hard times you face, it reveals what matters the most to you. Really allow God to speak to you through His word today as you read.

Prayer
What is God saying to you? What do you need to say to God? Use a prayer model and your monthly prayer targets and requests as a guide.

DAY 340

Worship
Get alone with God. Find a quiet place. Sit down. Silence all distractions.

Scripture: 2 Corinthians (10) (11) (12) (13)
In today's reading, you'll see that when a person's faith grows, the reach and spread of the gospel grows. It may seem like Paul is constantly correcting the Corinthians, but he does it from his revelation of who God is and what He can do for them if they fully obey and commit to God. Look for God's mercy throughout the scriptures today.

Prayer
What is God saying to you? What do you need to say to God? Use a prayer model and your monthly prayer targets and requests as a guide.

DAY 341

Worship
Get alone with God. Find a quiet place. Sit down. Silence all distractions.

Scripture: Romans ① ② ③
As you read today, you'll see God's passive wrath. This looks different than His active wrath you see in the Old Testament. Their actions have shown that their hearts are unrepentant. When you read today, ask and discover how this still displays God's character.

Prayer
What is God saying to you? What do you need to say to God? Use a prayer model and your monthly prayer targets and requests as a guide.

DAY 342

Worship
Get alone with God. Find a quiet place. Sit down. Silence all distractions.

Scripture: Romans ④ ⑤ ⑥ ⑦
At the end of the day, God isn't after our possessions, works, or words, He's after our hearts and obedience. When He sent Jesus to die for us, He made a direct connection from Him to us. In today's reading, look for God's generosity and grace.

Prayer
What is God saying to you? What do you need to say to God? Use a prayer model and your monthly prayer targets and requests as a guide.

DAY 343

Worship
Get alone with God. Find a quiet place. Sit down. Silence all distractions.

Scripture: Romans ⑧ ⑨ ⑩
The gospel is what we're called to share. It's the best news ever. Death doesn't need to be our ending, but eternal life is ours because of Jesus! God shows time and time again that He keeps His promises, and He includes everyone into His promises.

Prayer
What is God saying to you? What do you need to say to God? Use a prayer model and your monthly prayer targets and requests as a guide.

COMMUNITY

I attended a church service this week (circle):   YES   NO

I shared my faith and talked about my church with others this week (circle):   YES   NO

I connected with other Christians in a smaller group this week.
If yes, describe.

DAY 344

Worship
Get alone with God. Find a quiet place. Sit down. Silence all distractions.

Scripture: Romans (11) (12) (13)
Take a moment today and think about the last few days of reading and time spent with God. What have you learned? What are you discovering about God's character? What is God speaking to you about?

Prayer
What is God saying to you? What do you need to say to God? Use a prayer model and your monthly prayer targets and requests as a guide.

DAY 345

Worship
Get alone with God. Find a quiet place. Sit down. Silence all distractions.

Scripture: Romans (14) (15) (16)
When you read today, you'll see God's peace as the theme. Peace doesn't come naturally; we must pursue it by engaging the Spirit. We can't do this on our own, and we shouldn't want to. Engage the Spirit today. Pursue peace!

Prayer
What is God saying to you? What do you need to say to God? Use a prayer model and your monthly prayer targets and requests as a guide.

DAY 346

Worship
Get alone with God. Find a quiet place. Sit down. Silence all distractions.

Scripture: Acts (20) (21) (22) (23)
As you read today, consider how God is in every single detail, from Genesis to today's reading. God has lined everything up to work together for His plan! From the big details, to the tiny details that you may not even notice the first time you read through the Bible, we can see His plan unfolding as we near the end of our reading plan!

Prayer
What is God saying to you? What do you need to say to God? Use a prayer model and your monthly prayer targets and requests as a guide.

DAY 347

Worship
Get alone with God. Find a quiet place. Sit down. Silence all distractions.

Scripture: Acts (24) (25) (26)
In today's reading, Paul is left in prison and basically forgotten about for a few years. Paul has been through trial after trial and faced accusations and pain that we could not imagine. Through all of this, Paul has his eyes set on eternity and trusts God through every step. When you face trials and hardship, remember Paul's faithfulness and unwavering commitment to share the gospel.

Prayer
What is God saying to you? What do you need to say to God? Use a prayer model and your monthly prayer targets and requests as a guide.

DAY 348

Worship
Get alone with God. Find a quiet place. Sit down. Silence all distractions.

Scripture: Acts (27) (28)
In today's reading Paul (and the narrator of Acts, Luke), travel by ship to Rome to appeal to Caesar. Along the way, Paul is sharing the gospel and healing people. God is providing a way for the gospel to be spread no matter the circumstances that Paul faces.

Prayer
What is God saying to you? What do you need to say to God? Use a prayer model and your monthly prayer targets and requests as a guide.

DAY 349

Worship
Get alone with God. Find a quiet place. Sit down. Silence all distractions.

Scripture: Colossians (1) (2) (3) (4)   Philemon (1)
Today we read two books, Colossians and Philemon. Both books are letters written by Paul, the first to a church at Colossae, and the second is written to Philemon on behalf of Paul's good friend, Onesimus. To Colossae, Paul is encouraging them and giving guidance on some troubles they are facing. Lean in as Paul gives instruction on not only knowing but loving God and bearing fruit.

Prayer
What is God saying to you? What do you need to say to God? Use a prayer model and your monthly prayer targets and requests as a guide.

DAY 350

Worship
Get alone with God. Find a quiet place. Sit down. Silence all distractions.

Scripture: Ephesians ① ② ③ ④ ⑤ ⑥
Today we read Ephesians, a letter Paul wrote to churches in Ephesus. He gives general encouragement and instructions about the importance of unity in the body of Christ. Lean in as we read more wisdom from Paul about living out our faith.

Prayer
What is God saying to you? What do you need to say to God? Use a prayer model and your monthly prayer targets and requests as a guide.

COMMUNITY

I attended a church service this week (circle):   YES   NO

I shared my faith and talked about my church with others this week (circle):   YES   NO

I connected with other Christians in a smaller group this week.
If yes, describe.

DAY 351

Worship
Get alone with God. Find a quiet place. Sit down. Silence all distractions.

Scripture: Philippians ① ② ③ ④
Today we read another encouraging letter from Paul written to the church in Philippi. Philippians 4:6 says, "Don't worry about anything; instead, pray about everything. Tell God what you need, and thank him for all he has done." This is such a simple instruction that, when we follow it, can bring us so much peace!

Prayer
What is God saying to you? What do you need to say to God? Use a prayer model and your monthly prayer targets and requests as a guide.

DAY 352

Worship
Get alone with God. Find a quiet place. Sit down. Silence all distractions.

Scripture: 1 Timothy ① ② ③ ④ ⑤ ⑥
Today we read 1 Timothy, another letter from Paul Timothy is a leader at the church in Ephesus that Paul planted Timothy needs guidance in walking in humility and creating order while leading the church. We all need someone like Paul in our life, someone to share with us truth and instruction that honors God. As you read today, consider your relationships. Do you have someone like a Paul in your life?

Prayer
What is God saying to you? What do you need to say to God? Use a prayer model and your monthly prayer targets and requests as a guide.

DAY 353

Worship
Get alone with God. Find a quiet place. Sit down. Silence all distractions.

Scripture: Titus ① ② ③
Today we read Titus, a letter from Paul to his friend at the church in Crete. Lean into more wisdom from Paul as he gives Titus instruction for leading the church in a culture that goes against everything that Jesus teaches.

Prayer
What is God saying to you? What do you need to say to God? Use a prayer model and your monthly prayer targets and requests as a guide.

DAY 354

Worship
Get alone with God. Find a quiet place. Sit down. Silence all distractions.

Scripture: 1 Peter ① ② ③ ④ ⑤
Today we read 1 Peter, written to the gentiles in Rome. Peter is encouraging them and reminding them that God has chosen them, and to conduct themselves in a matter that catches the attention of other people. As followers of Christ, when we live in a way that makes others stop and wonder what is different, we lead people to Him.

Prayer
What is God saying to you? What do you need to say to God? Use a prayer model and your monthly prayer targets and requests as a guide.

DAY 355

Worship
Get alone with God. Find a quiet place. Sit down. Silence all distractions.

Scripture: Hebrews ① ② ③ ④ ⑤ ⑥
It's comforting knowing that God knows it all. Our past, present, and future. He's not surprised by what happens to you in life, though He may not have caused it, He has a plan to redeem your life. Notice how God is patient with us through these scriptures.

Prayer
What is God saying to you? What do you need to say to God? Use a prayer model and your monthly prayer targets and requests as a guide.

DAY 356

Worship
Get alone with God. Find a quiet place. Sit down. Silence all distractions.

Scripture: Hebrews ⑦ ⑧ ⑨ ⑩
Take time today before you read to ask God to reveal Himself through His word. Reflect on what you've learned and read over the last 355 days. God is doing something new today and wants you to come along. Be ready to receive.

Prayer
What is God saying to you? What do you need to say to God? Use a prayer model and your monthly prayer targets and requests as a guide.

DAY 357

Worship
Get alone with God. Find a quiet place. Sit down. Silence all distractions.

Scripture: Hebrews (11) (12) (13)
Today, we read about God as a rewarder. For everyone who has follows God and is faithful, He rewards them with more of Him. We can see the joy and excitement it brings to God when you read these scriptures. Look for it, you'll see His goodness and reward within the words!

Prayer
What is God saying to you? What do you need to say to God? Use a prayer model and your monthly prayer targets and requests as a guide.

COMMUNITY

I attended a church service this week (circle):   YES   NO

I shared my faith and talked about my church with others this week (circle):   YES   NO

I connected with other Christians in a smaller group this week.
If yes, describe.

DAY 358

Worship
Get alone with God. Find a quiet place. Sit down. Silence all distractions.

Scripture: 2 Timothy ① ② ③ ④
It's amazing to think that Paul, while expecting to be executed, still focused on the things that mattered to God. As you read today, be encouraged by the words Paul writes to Timothy. Even with words like suffering and persecution, God is there and still in control. God doesn't waste a moment.

Prayer
What is God saying to you? What do you need to say to God? Use a prayer model and your monthly prayer targets and requests as a guide.

DAY 359

Worship
Get alone with God. Find a quiet place. Sit down. Silence all distractions.

Scripture: 2 Peter ① ② ③   Jude ①
It's been a while but think about the Old Testament and the amount of times Jesus is foreshadowed. Now, think about the fact that Jesus has always existed. While you read today, remember that Jesus was and is, and is to come.

Prayer
What is God saying to you? What do you need to say to God? Use a prayer model and your monthly prayer targets and requests as a guide.

DAY 360

Worship
Get alone with God. Find a quiet place. Sit down. Silence all distractions.

Scripture: 1 John ① ② ③ ④ ⑤
In today's reading, it's simple and clear, God is love. Not only does He love us and shows His love for us, but He IS love. The only reason we can love Him at all is because it was His idea in the first place. Take that in today as you read. Soak in who He is and His love!

Prayer
What is God saying to you? What do you need to say to God? Use a prayer model and your monthly prayer targets and requests as a guide.

DAY 361

Worship
Get alone with God. Find a quiet place. Sit down. Silence all distractions.

Scripture: 2 John ①   3 John ①
God loves to go beyond human logic and reasoning to show is greatness. As you read today, notice how there are no boundaries that will get in the way of God's mission to pursue every living human on earth. Even those who claim to be His enemy. He still love them just as much as He loves you.

Prayer
What is God saying to you? What do you need to say to God? Use a prayer model and your monthly prayer targets and requests as a guide.

DAY 362

Worship
Get alone with God. Find a quiet place. Sit down. Silence all distractions.

Scripture: Revelation ① ② ③ ④ ⑤
We've arrived at the final book on our journey through the Bible together! Before you read today, ask God to help you approach this book with an open heart and His perspective on what He is doing with the scripture in today's context. Remember that much of this book was written through a lens that references Israel's history.

Prayer
What is God saying to you? What do you need to say to God? Use a prayer model and your monthly prayer targets and requests as a guide.

DAY 363

Worship
Get alone with God. Find a quiet place. Sit down. Silence all distractions.

Scripture: Revelation ⑥ ⑦ ⑧ ⑨ ⑩ ⑪
As you read today, look how God protects those who love and obey Him. Many people tend to fear the return of Jesus but as followers of Him, we should be expectant and excited for what that means for all of creation. It maybe the end times for the earth, but it's a new beginning for creation.

Prayer
What is God saying to you? What do you need to say to God? Use a prayer model and your monthly prayer targets and requests as a guide.

DAY 364

Worship
Get alone with God. Find a quiet place. Sit down. Silence all distractions.

Scripture: Revelation (12) (13) (14) (15) (16) (17) (18)
God is victorious, even before the battle can begin, He's already won. In today's reading, it can be pretty confusing. Just know that John's vision was probably seen through the lens of Israel's history. Everything that the enemy uses to come against the Kingdom of God fails, because a counterfeit will never outlast the authentic creation.

Prayer
What is God saying to you? What do you need to say to God? Use a prayer model and your monthly prayer targets and requests as a guide.

COMMUNITY

I attended a church service this week (circle):   YES   NO

I shared my faith and talked about my church with others this week (circle):   YES   NO

I connected with other Christians in a smaller group this week.
If yes, describe.

DAY 365

Worship

Get alone with God. Find a quiet place. Sit down. Silence all distractions.

Scripture: Revelation (19) (20) (21) (22)

Congratulations on making it to day 365! You read through the entire Bible in one year. You've learned about God's character and hopefully you have seen His work in your life as you've grown closer to him. Spend some extra time with Him today reflecting on how you've changed and how He has been faithful to you.

Prayer

What is God saying to you? What do you need to say to God? Use a prayer model and your monthly prayer targets and requests as a guide.

APPENDIX

BIBLE TRANSLATIONS

Word-For-Word   **Thought -For-Thought**   **Paraphrase**

Interlinear	NASB	ESV	KJV	HCSB	NAB	NIV	NCV	NIrV	CEV	MSG
	AMP	RSV	NKJV	NRSV	NJB	TNIV		NLT	GNT	TLB

NASB - New American Standard Bible

AMP - Amplified Bible

ESV - English Standard Version

RSV - Revised Standard Version

KJV - King James Version

NKJV - New King James Version

HCSB - Holman Christian Standard Bible

NRSV - New Revised Standard Version

NAB - New American Bible

NJB - New Jerusalem Bible

NIV - New International Version

TNIV - Today's New International Version

NCV - New Century Version

NLT - New Living Translation

NIrV - New International Reader's Version

GNT - Good News Translation

CEV - Contemporary English Version

TLB - The Living Bible

MSG - The Message

There are many excellent English Bible translations. They range between philosophies of translation that include 'Formal Equivalence' and 'Dynamic Equivalence.'

'Formal Equivalence' translations emphasize word-for-word accuracy and maintaining original grammar and syntax.

'Dynamic Equivalence' translations, in contrast, focus on translating the meaning of sentences and phrases without an emphasis on word-for-word accuracy, grammar, and syntax.

All translations employ both of these ideas in their philosophy. To some degree, with translation, there is always a trade-off between 'accuracy' and 'clarity.' Anyone who is bilingual knows that the 'best' translation is not always the most' literal.' It is best to pick a translation and then refer to other translations to gain a well-rounded understanding of the text.

Here is a breakdown of the different Bible translations:
Word For Word Translations use 'Formal Equivalence' translation exclusively to the degree possible.

Thought for Thought Translations use "Formal Equivalence" primarily unless "Dynamic Equivalence" is needed to translate the original meaning better.

Paraphrase Translations use "Dynamic Equivalence" to restate the text's meaning or passage using more modern words.

PRAYER MODELS

The Shema Prayer

Jesus likely would have prayed this famous prayer morning, noon, and night all His life.

> Hear, O Israel: The Lord our God, the Lord is one. Love the Lord your God
>
> with all your heart and with all your soul and with all your strength. These commandments that I give you today are to be on your hearts. Impress them on your children. Talk about them when you sit at home and when you walk along the road, when you lie down and when you get up.
>
> Tie them as symbols on your hands and bind them on your foreheads.
>
> Write them on the doorframes of your houses and on your gates.
>
> So if you faithfully obey the commands I am giving you today—to love the Lord your God and to serve him with all your heart and with all your soul—then I will send rain on your land in its season, both autumn and spring rains, so that you may gather in your grain, new wine and olive oil. I will provide grass in the fields for your cattle, and you will eat and be satisfied.
>
> Be careful, or you will be enticed to turn away and worship other gods and bow down to them. Then the Lord's anger will

burn against you, and he will shut up the heavens so that it will not rain and the ground will yield no produce, and you will soon perish from the good land the Lord is giving you.

Fix these words of mine in your hearts and minds; tie them as symbols on your hands and bind them on your foreheads. Teach them to your children, talking

about them when you sit at home and when you walk along the road, when you lie down and when you get up.

Write them on the doorframes of your houses and on your gates, so that your days and the days of your children may be many in the land the Lord swore to give your ancestors, as many as the days that the heavens are above the earth.

Deuteronomy 6:4-9; 11:13–21 NIV

The Armor Of God

God equips us with spiritual armor. Through prayer, we can stand against attacks of discouragement and doubt.

"Put on" the armor with this prayer based on Paul's exhortation in Ephesians 6:10–18, using God's Word, the sword of the Spirit, as we struggle, "not against flesh and blood, but against the powers of this dark world and against the spiritual forces of evil in the heavenly realms" (v. 12).

Equip me, Lord:
- **With the belt of truth** (v. 14). May your truth rule in my heart and be in my mind and on my lips today.
- **With the breastplate of righteousness** (v. 14). Apart from You there is no righteousness, but through Jesus I have been "born again" and made righteous in Your sight. May I live as a righteous person.
- **With feet fitted with the readiness that comes from the Gospel of peace** (v. 15). May I reflect the Gospel in my words and actions, that through me, with my every encounter, others may be drawn one step closer to You.
- **With the shield of faith** (v. 16). May I take You at Your word concerning promises about the present and future—promises of everlasting love, abundant life, and so much more.
- **With the helmet of salvation** (v. 17). Remind me that nothing can separate me from Your love and that I've been saved by grace. In Your grace, help me to say "no" to all ungodliness and worldly passions, and to live a self-controlled, upright, and godly life (Titus 2:12,13).
- **And with the sword of the Spirit, the Word of God** (v. 17). May Your Holy Spirit reign in my life and bring to my mind just the right Bible verses to be in my heart and on my lips. May I be "filled with the Spirit" and ready with Scripture as You were, Jesus, when the devil tempted You.
- **Finally, keep me in an attitude of prayer** (v. 18). Remind me to "pray in the Spirit on all occasions." Cause me to be alert and always praying for the saints; to be joyful and to give thanks in everything (see 1 Thessalonians 5:16-18).

The Tabernacle Of Prayer

In Exodus, Chapters 25 to 31, God gave detailed instructions to Moses on Mt. Sinai for building the Tabernacle to house His presence. The Tabernacle was a tent-like structure inside a rectangular courtyard, facing East, surrounded by a fence made of pillars and linen hangings, and covered an area 45' long and 15' wide with a 15' high covering.

In the outer courtyard, the brazen altar was closest to the entrance and the water's laver. Inside the tent was the Holy Place (housing the candlestick, the table of shewbread, and the golden altar of incense) and the Holy of Holies (where the Ark of the Covenant rested). In and above the Holy of Holies, God appeared as a pillar of cloud or fire. Each article of furniture represents a different prayer focus that has a unique meaning corresponding with its original purpose defined by God and a place in the "types and shadows" that exist between the Old and New Testaments.

Step 1: The Gate

Here, we enter into His gate with thanksgiving and into His courts with praise (Psalm 100:4)

Prayer Focus: We begin here. Thank God for every blessing and praise Him for His mighty acts.

Step 2: The Brazen Altar

For sinful man to even approach a holy God, there must be a blood sacrifice. Jesus died as an atonement for our sins. The brazen altar is where we repent and rid ourselves of our sinful deeds and desires.

Prayer Focus: No one can repent for us. Jesus became our sacrifice so we could receive the gift of repentance. At the altar, we search our hearts, acknowledge our sins, and ask God to forgive us.

Step 3: The Laver Of Water

Once sins were atoned for, cleansing was necessary before serving in the Holy Place. We must look into the mirror of; be washed by, and apply His Word as cleansing so we may serve and minister before Him.

Prayer Focus: Here we take time to read and meditate on God's Word and allow it to wash over us and through us. When we examine ourselves with His Word as our guide, the Word will sanctify and cleanse us.

Step 4: The Five Pillars
Each pillar symbolizes one of the characteristics of God named by Isaiah.

Prayer Focus: "His name shall be called Wonderful, Counselor, Mighty God, Everlasting Father and Prince of Peace" (Isaiah 9:6). Pray for revelation of the power of and for the office of each name to be present in our lives.

Step 5: The Golden Candlestick
This oil is symbolic of the illuminating and revelatory power of the Holy Ghost. The priest's duty was to keep the wicks trimmed so the lamp would exude pure light without smoke.

Prayer Focus: At this source of continuous shining light as God for spiritual revelation, direction, and guidance. Pray for the anointing of the Holy Ghost to be active in our lives. Jesus said, "I am the light of the world..." (John 8:12).

Step 6: The Table Of Showbread
The table/bread symbolized God's willingness to fellowship with man and him to be in His presence.

Prayer Focus: "I am the bread of life..." (John 6:35, 49-50) This bread of His presence is the "rhema" (God-breathed) Word of God to us. Ask God to speak to our hearts and allow us to commune with Him and hear His voice and follow Him. Pray for those who share His bread with us: missionaries, pastors, evangelists, and church leaders.

Step 7: The Golden Altar Of Incense
Only the fire of repentance can burn the incense of our intercession. This is a symbol of our prayers and intercession going up to God as a sweet fragrance.

Prayer Focus: "Let my prayer be set forth before thee as incense; and the lifting up of my hands as the evening sacrifice" (Psalm 141:2). Here the incense offered is symbolic of our worship. After worship, we make intercession for others and for any situation in our lives that requires His intervention. Biblically, Jesus makes intercession for us. The golden altar of incense is where every request can be presented to a prayer-answering God.

Step 8: The Veil

It represents the flesh of Jesus rent in the final sacrifice and marked physical separation from the spiritual. Whoever went into the Holy of Holies entered into God's very presence.

Prayer Focus: The veil is symbolic of the barrier of our flesh. Here we ask God to give us the power to go beyond ourselves, to operate not on our own faith but on God's faith. Meditate on the revelation of the name of JESUS and acknowledge Him as the Messiah- God manifest in the flesh as testified in the gospels. We enter into His presence.

Step 9: The Holy Of Holies

Inside the Holy of Holies was the Ark of the Covenant, which contained three symbolic items: a golden pot of manna, Aaron's staff that budded, and the stone containing the Ten Commandments. The Mercy Seat, where God communed with man, rested as the top of the ark. Because the ark was God's throne among His people, it was a symbol of His presence and power.

Prayer Focus: Only the blood gives us access to the Holy of Holies. The Ten Commandments (The Law) is covered by the blood of the sacrifice. There is only mercy. We are free and without judgment. This is the place of intimacy with God. Now we may act in the authority represented by Aaron's rod that budded. Through Christ, we take authority over things that will work against us. We are surrounded by angels, and the miracle of the manna reminds us that whatever we need, He will supply.

The Lord's Prayer

One way to pray like Jesus is to pray the Lord's Prayer word for word. You can also personalize it and use Jesus' words as a structure for your prayers. This post breaks the prayer down, verse by verse, so that you can pray like Jesus.

The Lord's Prayer is a passage from Jesus' longest, most detailed sermon. Here, Jesus gives us specific direction on how to pray. How amazing is that? This is the exact format for prayer that Jesus tells his disciples to use.

In addition to a formula, Jesus gives further direction in the verses prior to the Lord's Prayer. (Matthew 6: 5-8)

He tells us not to pray for the sake of impressing others but to pray in secret for our own reward. He also tells us not to be repetitive or to babble on and on as we pray. Our prayers do not need to be lengthy or extravagant, or wordy to be effective.

Step One: Start With Praise & Worship
"Our Father in heaven, hallowed be your name."

The word "hallowed" here means "honored as holy." The first step to any prayer is to give God glory and honor and praise. This positions our hearts to be aware of God's presence as we pray.

Here, Jesus also directs us to acknowledge God as our Father in Heaven. God is the creator of the universe, the alpha, and omega, the King of Kings, the Almighty. But, He is also our good, good Father who loves us and wants an intimate relationship with us.

Beginning prayer by calling him "Father" and praising His name brings us into His presence the right way, with reverence and awe, but also with intimacy and relationship.

You aren't just praying to a distant, powerful King. You are praying to the loving, tender God of your heart, who knows you fully and loves you deeply.

The words we choose have power; don't be hesitant or afraid to call Him your Heavenly Father.

Step Two: Pray God's Will Be Done
"Your kingdom come, your will be done, on earth as it is in heaven."

Jesus tells us to pray God's will over our own because the ultimate goal of prayer is not to convince God of our heart but to align it with His. Praying God's will to be done in our situation puts His agenda before our own.

This is the mark of a truly surrendered heart. We can certainly pray specifically for our hearts' desires; He knows them anyway. But ultimately, our main desire should be for God's will to prevail.

Even if His will is the opposite of our desire. Even more specifically, Jesus instructs us to pray God's will to be done on earth as it is in Heaven. What does this mean?

It means that we desire His will to be done freely, without disobedience or obstacle or hindrance of human sin. Jesus tells us to pray this way not because God needs us to do His will, but because He chooses to use us to do the work of His Kingdom.

To do His good work, we have to trust Him and obey Him while striving to deny our sinful human nature. In Heaven, these issues are not present. But on earth, they are.

We should desire His will to be done and for us to not stand in the way of it by disobeying or sinning.

Step Three: Pray For Your Needs
"Give us this day our daily bread,"

Here, Jesus transitions into instructing us to pray for the provision of our needs, no matter how seemingly insignificant or mundane.

We need daily bread in the sense that we need God to daily dwell with us and guide us, but also that we need literal daily bread to stay alive.

Pray for both His physical and spiritual provision in your life, and he lives of those you love.

God created us with bodies and souls that both need daily substance to sustain them. Pray for the things that you need and thank Him for all that He has already blessed you with.

Step Four: Confess Sin & Ask For Forgiveness
"..and forgive us our debts,"

Many times when we pray, we forget these next two steps, but they are vitally important to our walk with God.

We need to regularly ask God to search our hearts and reveal our sin to us. We need to regularly be confessing those sins to God and asking Him to forgive us.

Prayer is about cultivating a relationship with Jesus, and in any relationship, part of intimacy is humility and openness. Humble, open, teachable hearts apologize when they are wrong.

The mark of a truly humble heart is a genuine desire to apologize for wrongdoing and seek forgiveness.

Do not leave any sin unconfessed; unrepented sin erodes relationship with God and hinders intimacy with Him.

Ask the Lord to search your heart and reveal an unrepented sin to you.

Step Five: Ask For Help Forgiving Others
"..as we also have forgiven our debtors."

You may not think that you regularly need to forgive others, but this doesn't just refer to obvious conflicts. This can mean forgiving someone for disappointing you or letting you down as well as forgiving someone who has wronged you.

The way we talk about others and post on social media should show you how badly we need the help of the Holy Spirit to continually offer forgiveness to others.

We should offer it freely, whether it is deserved or requested, because we have been forgiven when we did not deserve it.

It is our duty as Christians to portray the love of Christ to the world, and this means forgiving when the world would say retribution is justified. This means forgiving those who slander you or speak against you when the world would say they don't deserve your kindness.

This is not an easy task. Our flesh will fight against this tooth and nail, so we need to regularly pray for the strength to forgive others.

Step Six: Pray For Safety, Protection & Deliverance
"And lead us not into temptation, but deliver us from evil."

Though God allows us to be tempted and tested, He is never the tempter (James 1:13-14). We lead ourselves into situations where we are tempted. Here Jesus is showing us how to pray against this and keep us from being our own worst enemy.

This part of prayer is important because our flesh is weak against temptation. Though we can withstand and overcome through the strength of God (Philippians 4:13), it is better if we can steer clear of temptation from the beginning.

We should also pray that we do not cause temptation for any other brother or sister in Christ.

Pray also here for protection and safety, as we have a real enemy who lives to attack God's people. Pray, as Jesus says, for "deliverance from evil."

The Prayer Of Jabez

Scripture has many examples of prayers that teach us to depend on God and call upon Him. The prayer of Jabez is very inspiring and challenging for how we approach God with our requests. 2 Timothy 3:16-17 tells us that "ALL Scripture is God-breathed and is useful for teaching, rebuking, and training in righteousness, so that the servant of God may be thoroughly equipped for every good work."

Jabez was not using prayer as a formula to get something from God; rather, He was calling upon God to help him accomplish the promises of God! Let's dive in and see how this Old Testament prayer can be applied today as we seek God's provision and leading in our lives.

The Prayer of Jabez Text, 1 Chronicles 4:10
"Jabez cried out to the God of Israel, "Oh that You would bless me and enlarge my territory! Let your hand be with me, and keep me from harm so that I will be free from pain." And God granted his request."

The Prayer of Jabez Meaning & Lessons
1. The very first thing Scripture tells us about Jabez is that he cried to the God of Israel. Jabez states God's lordship and headship over his life. When you pray, begin by acknowledging who God is!

2. "That you would bless me" Jabez not only recognizes God as the one and only true God, he also acknowledges that blessings come from God alone. Are you chasing broken promises and blessings that the world tries to entice you with? Are you striving toward prosperity on your own strength? When you pray, do it with a heart fully invested in the blessings of God.

3. "that you would multiply my territory" – Many think that Jabez is simply referring to physical land when asking to multiply territory. However, if we look at the lineage of Jabez, we can understand that he is not merely speaking in terms of wealth and prosperity but in terms of impacting the kingdom of God. He wanted his spiritual territory to increase, to claim generations for the Lord of Israel. Do you need to claim or reclaim some of the land Satan has taken from you? When you pray, ask God to multiply your territory and to do more through you!

4. "your hand be with me" – Jabez wanted God to be in every moment of his day. He understood the power of God's hand to protect and to lead in the right direction. Blessings will become curses if it is not God's hand providing and guiding. When you pray, request more than blessings and provision but that God's hand would lead you through any circumstances and trials that come your way. THAT is the greatest blessing.

5. "keep me from harm so that I will be free from pain" The name Jabez literally means "born with pain." His own mother named him this because of the pain she endured in labor! When Jabez prays, he speaks against the testimony of his name and lets go of the shame it covered him in. When you pray, come to God vulnerable and ready for Him to turn your weakness into His glory.

When we learn to submit our will to God and pray like Jabez, we will begin to see God move in mighty ways! What are you praying for today?

Berakhot

Berakhot are prayers of blessing that were a part of worship gatherings during Jesus' day. While some of the nuances adapted over the years, Jesus would have prayed a version of these prayers.

Morning
When you first wake up and open your eyes.
"Blessed is He who gives sight to the blind."
When you get out of bed.
"Blessed is He who sets the captives free."
When you get dressed.
"Blessed is He who clothes the naked."
When you put on your shoes.
"Blessed is He who provides for all my needs."

Throughout Your Day
When you eat a meal where bread is at the table, you hold up the bread and say...
"Blessed is He who brings forth bread from the earth."
When you eat a meal where wine is at the table.
"Blessed is He, Creator of the fruit of the vine."
When you eat a meal any other types of foods.
"Blessed is He through whose word all things come"
When you see the first budding tree in springtime.
"Blessed is He who did not omit anything from the world, And created it with good creations and good trees for people to enjoy."
When you see lightning, falling stars, mountains, great deserts, or the sky in its beauty.
"Blessed is He who made the creation."
When you hear thunder or feel an earthquake.
"Blessed is He whose strength and power fill the world."
When you see a beautiful person, animal, or tree.
"Blessed is He who has such as these in the world."

On Certain Occasions
When you see a friend after a year's separation.
"Blessed is He who revives the dead."

When it rains, or something else good happens.
"Blessed is He who is good and gives good things."
When something terrible happens..
"Blessed is He who is the one true judge."
When you are saved from an accident or serious illness.
"Blessed is He who does good to the undeserving and has rendered every kindness to me."
When you encounter a place where God has done a miracle.
"Blessed is He who has done miracles in this place."
When you reach a highly anticipated happy occasion.
"Blessed is He who has given us life, and preserved us, and brought us to this season."

The Amidah

The Amidah is a prayer that was a part of worship gatherings during Jesus' day. While they have adapted over the years, Jesus would have prayed blessings such as these.

You are mighty forever, O Lord, you resurrect the dead, you are great to save. Sustaining the living in the loving-kindness, resurrecting the dead in abundant mercy, You support the falling and heal the sick, set free the captives, and keep the faith of those who sleep in the dust. Who is like you, Master of mighty deeds, and who may be compared to You? O King, who sends death and revives again, and causes salvation to sprout. You are surely believed to resurrect the dead.

You are holy, and Your name is holy, and the holy ones praise Your name every day. Blessed are You, O Lord, the Holy God.

You graciously give knowledge to man and give mortals understanding. Favor us with your knowledge, understanding, and intelligence. Blessed are You, O Lord, who graciously gives understanding.

Bless for us, O Lord our God, this year and all its yield for good, and shower down a blessing on the earth. Fill us with Your bounty and bless our year that it be as the good years. Blessed are You, O Lord, who blesses the years.

Restore our judges as before, and our counselors as in the beginning, and remove from us grief and sighing. Reign over us, O Lord, You alone, in loving-kindness and compassion, and clear us in judgment. Blessed are You, O Lord, the King, who loves righteousness and judgment.

Hear our voice, O Lord our God, spare and have mercy on us and accept in mercy and favor our prayer, for You are a God who hears prayers and supplications. Do not turn us away empty-handed, O our King, when we come before You, for You listen to the prayer of Your people Israel in mercy. Blessed are You, O Lord, who hears prayer.

We acknowledge to You, O Lord, that You are our God as You were the God to the God of our fathers, forever and ever. Rock of our life, Shield our salvation, You are unchanging from age to age. We thank You and declare Your praise for our lives that are in Your hands and for our souls that are entrusted to You. Your miracles are with us every day, and your benefits are with us at all times, evening and morning and midday. You are good, for your mercies are endless; You are merciful for Your kindness are never complete; from everlasting, we have hoped in You. And for all these things may Your name be blessed and exalted, always and forevermore.

Let every living thing give thanks to you and praise Your name in truth, O God, our salvation and our help. Blessed are You, O Lord, Your name is good, and to you, it is right to give thanks.

OTHER RECOMMENDED RESOURCES

Better: My Life. God's Design.
by Stephen Martin

We want "better," and we want it now.

Americans spend billions of dollars every year in our efforts to get better. We want to be better today than we were yesterday and better tomorrow than we are today. We want next year to be better than last.
We're worried that we're not good enough and, no matter how hard we try, we can never measure up to everyone's expectations. We want to be better people, better friends, better husbands or wives, better parents. We want "better," and we want it now.

But what if the key to "better" isn't what we think it is? What if it doesn't start with us at all?

What if our concept of "better" isn't good enough?

With its essential life-application principles and in-depth personal and group study materials, *Better: My Life. God's Design.* by Stephen Martin is designed to help you learn the keys to "better" and discover that, with God's help, the better life you want is within your reach.

Order your copy of the book *Better: My Life. God's Design.* wherever books are sold.

OTHER RECOMMENDED RESOURCES

Wiser: How To Build And Manage Wealth God's Way
by Stephen Martin

Richer. Winner. Owner. Wealthier. Happier.

Whenever we think about our finances, those are some of the words that usually come to mind. If you want to be a winner in this world, you need to have a big house, a big car, and a big paycheck. Right? Everyone thinks that having more money and owning more stuff naturally makes you happier in life.

But what if everyone is wrong?

What if happiness isn't really tied to the number of things you possess, the size of your bank account, or what you can claim ownership over in this life? What if the key to becoming happier with our personal finances and possessions was found in just one word? Wiser.

Building wealth and leaving a legacy that makes a real impact in this world isn't just about becoming richer. It's about becoming WISER. It's about understanding four important biblical principles and applying them practically in our lives. As we learn and practice the four foundational truths presented in this book, we'll discover that building and stewarding our resources God's way will bring us true and lasting wealth.

Order your copy of the book ***Wiser: How To Build And Manage Wealth God's Way*** wherever books are sold.

OTHER RECOMMENDED RESOURCES

The **Better Planner**™ is a thirteen-week personal planner designed to help you map out all the different aspects of success and personal growth on your way to better.

It can get complicated to make sure you're doing all the right things in all the right areas of life, but the **Better Planner**™ cuts through all the confusing apps and habit trackers and puts the path to personal development right into the palm of your hands.

The **Better Planner**™ is radically different in its approach. By incorporating the seven biblical principles found in the book **Better: My Life. God's Design.** into one easy-to-use, thirteen-week planner, the **Better Planner**™ provides a framework for you to achieve success and follow God's plan for your life.
The foundation of the **Better Planner**™ is the practice of defining and reaching your personal vision. The other principles for growth all integrate with and flow out of this essential step.

As you develop and record the insights you receive from God and His design for your life, the **Better Planner**™ will lead you through a step-by-step process to become better.

To start your journey to better, order your copy of the **Better Planner**™ at *betterplanner.com* today!

OTHER RECOMMENDED RESOURCES

Start Here: An Introduction To The Gospel, The Holy Spirit And The Local Church
by Stephen Martin

Start Here: An Introduction To The Gospel, The Holy Spirit And The Local Church, is designed to help you jump-start your faith by getting to know God through His Word, the Bible.

With everything surrounding us today, it can be hard to know where to start, especially in regard to following Jesus. Start Here is a 21-day guided devotional where you will learn three essentials that form the foundation of the Christian life: The Gospel, The Holy Spirit and The Local Church. You will spend seven days focusing on each of these essentials as you continue to grow in your faith over time.

ABOUT THE AUTHOR

Stephen Martin has been in ministry, serving the local church for more than twenty years. Born and raised in Tulsa, Oklahoma, Stephen began serving in ministry as a teenager, and then as an intern at his hometown church, Church On The Move. He went on to help with a local church plant and earn a bachelor's degree in interdisciplinary studies from Lindenwood University in Saint Louis, Missouri.

Stephen is passionate about serving and resourcing the local church—specifically church leaders. In 2009, he started One Church Resource, a global, online, sharing network for pastors, church leaders, and creatives.

In 2013, Stephen and his family moved to Texas and planted Vintage Church just outside of Fort Hood, the largest military base in the United States. Today, Vintage Church is a church of thousands and continues to make a significant impact in the Central Texas region. As the founder and Senior Pastor of this vibrant, growing congregation, Stephen firmly believes in its mission of *Reaching People and Building Family*. He is dedicated to helping others take steps to grow into their God-given potential.

When he's not pastoring people or coaching leaders, Stephen loves spending time with his family, hunting deer, and reading. Stephen's wife, Kyla, is a Family Medicine Physician, and they have two beautiful daughters, Adilyn and Breelyn, and two sons, Greyson and Colton.

PRAYER TARGETS

Month: _____   Year: _____

My Family

_____
_____
_____

My Church

_____
_____
_____

My Relationships

_____
_____
_____

My Sphere Of Influence

_____
_____
_____

My Spiritual Growth

_____
_____
_____

PRAYER REQUESTS

Date	Person's Name	Prayer Requests/Praise Reports

PRAYER TARGETS

Month: _____   Year: _____

My Family

_____

_____

_____

My Church

_____

_____

_____

My Relationships

_____

_____

_____

My Sphere Of Influence

_____

_____

_____

My Spiritual Growth

_____

_____

_____

PRAYER REQUESTS

Date	Person's Name	Prayer Requests/Praise Reports

PRAYER TARGETS

Month: _____ Year: _____

My Family

_____

_____

_____

My Church

_____

_____

_____

My Relationships

_____

_____

_____

My Sphere Of Influence

_____

_____

_____

My Spiritual Growth

_____

_____

_____

PRAYER REQUESTS

Date	Person's Name	Prayer Requests/Praise Reports

PRAYER TARGETS

Month: _____   Year: _____

My Family

_____

_____

_____

My Church

_____

_____

_____

My Relationships

_____

_____

_____

My Sphere Of Influence

_____

_____

_____

My Spiritual Growth

_____

_____

_____

PRAYER REQUESTS

Date	Person's Name	Prayer Requests/Praise Reports

PRAYER TARGETS

Month: _____   Year: _____

My Family

_____

_____

_____

My Church

_____

_____

_____

My Relationships

_____

_____

_____

My Sphere Of Influence

_____

_____

_____

My Spiritual Growth

_____

_____

_____

PRAYER REQUESTS

Date	Person's Name	Prayer Requests/Praise Reports

PRAYER TARGETS

Month: _____   Year: _____

My Family

_____

_____

_____

My Church

_____

_____

_____

My Relationships

_____

_____

_____

My Sphere Of Influence

_____

_____

_____

My Spiritual Growth

_____

_____

_____

PRAYER REQUESTS

Date	Person's Name	Prayer Requests/Praise Reports

PRAYER TARGETS

Month: _____ Year: _____

My Family

_____

_____

_____

My Church

_____

_____

_____

My Relationships

_____

_____

_____

My Sphere Of Influence

_____

_____

_____

My Spiritual Growth

_____

_____

_____

PRAYER REQUESTS

Date	Person's Name	Prayer Requests/Praise Reports

PRAYER TARGETS

Month: _____   Year: _____

My Family

_____

_____

_____

My Church

_____

_____

_____

My Relationships

_____

_____

_____

My Sphere Of Influence

_____

_____

_____

My Spiritual Growth

_____

_____

_____

PRAYER REQUESTS

Date	Person's Name	Prayer Requests/Praise Reports

PRAYER TARGETS

Month: _____ Year: _____

My Family

_____

_____

_____

My Church

_____

_____

_____

My Relationships

_____

_____

_____

My Sphere Of Influence

_____

_____

_____

My Spiritual Growth

_____

_____

_____

PRAYER REQUESTS

Date	Person's Name	Prayer Requests/Praise Reports

PRAYER TARGETS

Month: _____   Year: _____

My Family

_____
_____
_____

My Church

_____
_____
_____

My Relationships

_____
_____
_____

My Sphere Of Influence

_____
_____
_____

My Spiritual Growth

_____
_____
_____

PRAYER REQUESTS

Date	Person's Name	Prayer Requests/Praise Reports

PRAYER TARGETS

Month: _____   Year: _____

My Family

_____

_____

_____

My Church

_____

_____

_____

My Relationships

_____

_____

_____

My Sphere Of Influence

_____

_____

_____

My Spiritual Growth

_____

_____

_____

PRAYER REQUESTS

Date	Person's Name	Prayer Requests/Praise Reports

PRAYER TARGETS

Month: _____   Year: _____

My Family

_____

_____

_____

My Church

_____

_____

_____

My Relationships

_____

_____

_____

My Sphere Of Influence

_____

_____

_____

My Spiritual Growth

_____

_____

_____

PRAYER REQUESTS

Date	Person's Name	Prayer Requests/Praise Reports

Made in the USA
Coppell, TX
22 December 2020